Sharing

the

Children

Sharing

the

Children

How to Resolve Custody Problems
and Get on with Your Life

ROBERT E. ADLER, Ph.D.

ADLER&ADLER

306.89
Ad 5

Published in the United States
in 1988 by
Adler & Adler, Publishers, Inc.
4550 Montgomery Avenue
Bethesda, Maryland 20814

Library of Congress Cataloging-in-Publication Data
Adler, Robert E., 1946–
Sharing the children.

Bibliography: p.
Includes index.
1. Children of divorced parents—United States.   2. Joint custody of
children—United States.   I. Title.
HQ777.5.A34   1988
646.7'8   87-19532
ISBN 0-917561-50-3

Printed in the United States of America
First edition

To my parents,
without whose love
this book would never have been written,
and to my wife, Jo Ann Wexler,
without whom it might have been written sooner,
but with much less love.

Contents

Acknowledgments

The many children and parents whose love, sensitivity, and courage inspired me throughout this endeavor deserve my deepest thanks. Their names, of course, have been changed for the purposes of this book. They were my real teachers about living through divorce; I hope that I have been able to pass on some of their experience and wisdom while respecting their privacy.

Nancy Peterson's insightful review and analysis of the psychological literature was of immeasurable help in building the foundation of this book. *Sharing the Children* would still be a dream without her contribution. Thanks also to H. James Toland III of the Bureau of National Affairs, Inc., for his up-to-the-minute research on custody laws throughout the United States.

The work of many gifted researchers and clinicians has enriched this book. I am particularly grateful to Constance Ahrons, Diana Baumrind, Linda E. G. Campbell, Stella Chess, William F. Hodges, Dorothy Huntington, Janet R. Johnston, Joan B. Kelly, Alan M. Levy, Isolina Ricci, Dianne Skafte, Ann Kaiser Stearns, Mary C. Tall, Alexander Thomas, Judith S. Wallerstein, and Lenore Weitzman; they have brilliantly illuminated what would otherwise be obscure.

Special thanks to the Honorable Rex H. Sater, who stands as a model of a humane and enlightened judge, and who took the time to help me to understand the goals and process of family law from the bench. Thanks also to the Honorable Patricia Bresee. Her great compassion for children shines through all of her work as attorney and judge.

My appreciation goes to Michael Lentz, whose extraordinary

accomplishments as director of the Sonoma County Family Mediation Services helped me to see how well divorcing families can be served by an innovative and flexible court system. Thanks also to Herbert Larsen II, whose work shows that warmth and patience are of value even in the toughest and most time-limited mediations.

Gary Friedman, attorney and mediator, continues to be an invaluable teacher and model in the area of mediation. I thank him for demonstrating time and again that seemingly intractable conflicts can be resolved by those willing to go deep enough to discover the values they share. Another model is Michael N. Nagler, who has deepened my understanding of nonviolence in action. My deepest thanks to Eknath Easwaran, who lives what he teaches.

Many attorneys have given generously of their time and experience to contribute to this book. Special thanks to Amy Rodney and Larry Moskowitz, and to Chris Anderson, Jan Burland, Greg Jilka, Steven Neustadter, Trish Nugent, and Kate Nowell.

Charles Villarreal and Thomas J. Brady gave me the opportunity to work closely with court officers charged with the task of evaluating families in custody disputes. Kristina Foster, Jeanne Ingenito, and R. Mark Williams taught me at least as much about this most difficult endeavor as I taught them, and for this I thank them.

Rosemarie Bolen, Jim Gumina, Albert Kastl, Tony Madrid, Xavier McPhee, Judy Reed, and Roger Rose are some of the many therapists whose work with divorcing families has inspired and shaped my understanding. I thank them for sharing their experience and expertise with me.

The Institute, and particularly Lou Miller, has provided continuing encouragement, challenge, and diversion. My family—Hy S. Adler, Les and Judith Adler, and my wife Jo Ann Wexler—has inspired and supported me in ways too numerous to count.

Literary agents Michael Larson and Elizabeth Pomada have guided me from the earliest stages of this work. I appreciate their professionalism, style, and personal touch. In particular, they guided *Sharing the Children* into the hands of Jim and Esthy Adler. I am extremely grateful to my editors Amy Pastan and Madelyn Larsen; every suggestion they made has resulted in a better book.

CHAPTER I
Life after Divorce

In my practice I have worked with many people in pain. I have counseled people who have fled from political oppression, concentration camp victims, schizophrenics and their families. I have listened to men and women in deep depression. People have told me of their frustration, helplessness, and rage at the illness and death of their parents, their children, or their mates. Parents of children born autistic, brain damaged, or developmentally delayed have spoken of their years of struggle and heartbreak. In their words, drawings, and play, children have conveyed to me their histories of neglect and abuse.

Surprisingly, from among these many unhappy people, one group stands out as among the most confused, the most trapped, and the most hurt and helpless. These are divorced or divorcing parents caught in a seemingly endless pattern of resentment, animosity, and pain. The months or years that have passed since they separated have not healed their wounds. The shock of betrayal, the humiliation they felt, their sense of loss and victimization, remain as vivid as if they had happened yesterday. They continue to seethe with anger, leading them to avoid all contact with each other or to make every meeting a tense, hostile standoff. For some, periods of uneasy truce are punctuated by explosive exchanges of crtiticism, threats, and, all too often, violence. These parents and their children are trapped in a continuing struggle, a hot or cold war that has taken on a life of its own, poisoning years of their lives.

When parents divorce, their family does not die; like a living cell, it splits in two. At its best the result is a new kind of family with surprising structure, a healthy, thriving organism with two separate, equally vital centers. No matter how severe their initial

1

problems, most families do achieve this kind of transformation over time, allowing parents and children to go on to live fulfilling lives on their own terms.

Although the details of their custody arrangements vary greatly, those divorced parents who go on to lead fulfilling lives share several key traits: they have let go of the past and are busy and involved with new people, activities, and relationships. They have developed independent lives and have stopped trying to control and interfere with each other. They have shown their children that it is safe and acceptable to love both of them. As a result, the children have a loving, realistic relationship with both parents. Finally, these parents, despite their divorce and their continuing differences, have developed a businesslike, workable way of dealing with each other when it comes to the children.

Many families, however, do not make it across the divorce and child custody minefield safely. The statistics vary, but experts report that one-quarter to one-half of all divorced families continue to live with destructive levels of friction, hostility, and bitterness, even years after separating. Their lawyers call them "hostility junkies." Psychologists describe them as entrenched in intractable disputes. Teachers find their children troubled, depressed, and prone to school failure and antisocial behavior.

When I first started working with families like these I was sure that the root of these severe, chronic problems had to lie in psychological flaws of one or both parents. I thought that horror stories like those I heard could never happen unless one or both of the parents were seriously disturbed. To my surprise I found that these men and women could not be distinguished from parents who had worked out their custody problems far more successfully, or from parents who had never divorced.

As I learned about their backgrounds and how they were managing other aspects of their lives, I discovered that most of them were neither bad people nor emotionally disturbed. They differed not so much in *who* they were, but in *what* had happened to them and in *how* they had gone about trying to solve their problems. It was the specifics of what they had experienced, said, and done while trying to separate and divorce that had gotten them in trouble, not the kind of people they were.

Gradually, I came to see separation and divorce for most people as a dangerous journey, like crossing a flooded river or traversing a ledge across the face of a treacherous cliff. With care, persistence, and luck, many parents are able to make it across with their own and their children's lives intact. However, many other parents, equally well motivated, are blinded by emotional storms or trapped in endless battles, preventing them from solving the urgent problem of just getting through safely. These people, bogged down in endless bitterness and resentment, battered by repeated litigation, are not helped by criticism or condemnation. They need to know how to go forward again, along with a clear understanding of the territory they have to cross and the means to reach their goal.

Sharing the Children is meant to provide that aid. It is based on the belief that you, like every divorcing parent, want to build a better life for yourself and your children. It is designed to provide you with the knowledge and skills other divorcing parents have used to work out successful solutions to their divorce and custody problems, despite the obstacles that make that goal so hard to reach.

This book offers two keys to help you work out realistic, livable solutions to your divorce and custody problems. The first is a solid understanding of what separating, divorcing, and rebuilding a family are all about. The second is "know how," a straightforward and consistent way of dealing with feelings, communicating, and acting that works in this complex and threatening new world.

In working with divorcing parents I have realized that information and suggestions, however helpful, are not enough. Although some parents have all the skills they need to work things out, most need to learn new ways of looking at their situations and new methods for dealing constructively with them. The checklists and examples in the following chapters are designed to help you turn good ideas into useful skills. Reading this book can help you to understand what is going on, to look at your problems constructively, and to communicate and act effectively. I hope you will make its ideas your own and put them to work for you and your children.

CHAPTER 2

From Conflict to Cooperation

My ex-husband and I are not competing against each other for the
children—we're trying as hard as we can to work together so that we
can give the kids what they need without giving up what we need.
—Elizabeth

The biggest obstacle for parents and children following divorce, the main hindrance preventing them from creating happy new lives, is intractable conflict—a pattern of powerful feelings of betrayal, hurt, anger, and fear stimulated by, and in turn causing, continuing hostilities between the parents. These families do not find a new life after divorce; instead, the divorce becomes their life.

In contrast, many families emerge from the crisis of divorce with secure, thriving children and with two parents who are able to get on with their lives. These are families in which everyone wins, not because one parent defeats the other—a "victory" that can only mean pain for the children—but because both parents have been able to work together to overcome the destructive forces of divorce.

In these successful families, both parents are able to let go of the past, create independent lifestyles, and pursue their own goals. Their children are free to love both parents and are assured of meaningful relationships with them. This three-way victory, in which mother, father, and children all come out ahead, is achieved when parents complete their emotional divorce, gain realistic autonomy, yet balance their own needs for independence with their children's need for them to work together.

Many divorced parents, however, never experience either the true independence of adults living their own lives or the businesslike cooperation needed to raise healthy children. Many cannot even imagine this kind of success for themselves and their children—they are caught in hostile competition, trapped by a win-lose view of divorce. As long as either winning or losing is the only way they can see their situation, they may never find adequate solutions to their problems.

The Win-Lose Worldview: A Blueprint for Failure

We are all familiar with win-lose thinking. We casually label people we know as winners or losers, as if all of life were a game. Politicians, businessmen, and advertisers deliberately use the win-lose imagery of sports and war because it is powerful and easily understood. However, because this way of looking at events and people is so pervasive, we often fail to see that cooperation is an essential part of even the most highly competitive situations. Sports, politics, business, and law all appear highly competitive, yet they are all based on intricate systems of agreements and rules arrived at cooperatively. A win-lose mindset easily blinds us to the many situations where cooperation, not competition, is the only successful approach. It would be impossible to carry out any meaningful enterprise, negotiate a contract, or even drive across town, without the cooperation of many different people. Even if win-lose thinking is useful for dealing with certain highly competitive areas of life, it can be very destructive where independent action, cooperation, or nurturance are needed.

With amazing regularity, research contradicts the assumption that competition brings out the best in people and is essential for high productivity and excellence. Robert Helmreich and Janet Spence, social scientists at the University of Texas, write that this body of research "dramatically refutes the contention that competitiveness is vital to a successful business career." In education, in scientific achievement, in a variety of work situations as well as in business, studies over the last thirty-five years have shown clearly that high levels of achievement go hand in hand with high levels of cooperation, and that high levels of competition actually reduce achievement. The win-lose way of structuring the world inevitably perpetuates conflict. Yesterday's defeated loser almost always reappears as today's angry avenger. How many of the world's most serious problems are the results of previous "victories"?

Win-lose thinking is especially dangerous in the intimate, vulnerable world of a family. Decisive victories, those moments in which an angry spouse can say, "I really showed him," or, "She finally got what's coming to her," seldom end the war. A battle may be won or lost, but there is almost always another round where the roles of victim and victor may be reversed— and always at the expense of the children.

One angry woman I know kept going back to court for more and more support. She finally won a big victory—a judge gave her the satisfaction of a court order that fulfilled her desire to get back at her ex-husband. Her vindication, however, lasted less than twenty-four hours. The same day the order was issued, her ex-husband broke a rule at work and lost his job. He was back in court a few weeks later, "winning" a drastic reduction of support. It is hard to see either of these parents as victors, but it is easy to see that both of them, and their children, lost.

To emerge from the pain and confusion of divorce feeling good about yourself, your family, and your future, you must be clear about your goals, about what you really want for yourself and your children. If you and your ex-spouse become trapped in win-lose thinking, your entire family risks years of destructive conflict. If instead you can substitute win-win thinking, consistently searching for solutions that work for everyone, you can join the many families for whom divorce marks the beginning of a new life as much as the end of the old.

How Children Can Win

Children win when they have a secure and close relationship with both parents.

Todd, a tall, personable, and good-looking ten-year-old, seemed to have everything going for him. He had a good sense of humor and could talk easily about himself and his interests. His teachers said he was bright. I found it hard to believe what his mother told me—that he was unhappy and isolated at school and frequently shocked her and his friends with his angry explosions. She brought him to me for therapy when he started saying that he should never have been born.

I talked to Todd after one of his bad days, a day when he had gotten into a fight with his teacher and "walked away" from school.

"What happened?" I asked.

"Nothing happened."

"I thought maybe someone said something to you, hurt your feelings, made you mad?"

"No, nothing like that."

"Sometimes kids get upset when something happens at home."

"No, it was just regular at home."

"I sometimes get sad or mad just thinking about something. Does that ever happen to you?"

"Yeah, a lot."

"Was that what happened today?"

"I guess so."

"What were you thinking about?"

"My Dad." Todd wiped his eye with the back of his hand. "You know, I don't even know where he is."

Todd is one of the hundreds of children I have worked with whose lives were stunted because of the loss of a parent through divorce. Like a botched surgery, their parents' divorce left a hole in their lives, sometimes an open wound, but more often a gap healed over, emptiness denied but not forgotten.

Children need continuing, high-quality contact with both parents. Few psychological findings have so much evidence to support them. At least fifteen research studies have shown that even years after the divorce, the quality of the children's contact with both parents is central to their well-being. In a representative study, Robert Hess and Kathleen Camara found that children who were able to maintain good relationships with both parents were less stressed by divorce, showed less anger and aggression, and got along better with others than children who had poorer relations with one of their divorced parents. After studying divorced families for over ten years, Wallerstein and Kelly emphasized, "Regardless of the legal allocation of responsibility and custody, the emotional significance of the relationship with each of two parents did not diminish [over time]."

Active involvement with both parents is a critical determinant of how children feel about the divorce, their parents, and themselves, all of their lives.

Children win when they are protected from their parents' conflicts, and when parents handle their own conflicts well.

What does involvement in parental hostilities do to children? The research findings are sobering:

- Men whose fathers were wife batterers have a 1000% higher incidence of wife abuse than other men.
- Women whose mothers were abused are more likely to enter physically abusive relationships and less likely to get out of them than other women.
- Children who experience family violence are 2.5 times more likely to show serious behavior problems than children from nonviolent homes; as adults they have a much higher incidence of adjustment problems.
- Children who are abducted from one parent by another suffer severe emotional damage. Dorothy Huntington, a psychologist who has studied and helped many of these "milk carton kids," says flatly, "Most kidnappings occur out of revenge against the other spouse, not out of love for the child. If a child is gone very long, there will be major impacts. Children can become very frightened about going out of the house, afraid the kidnap is going to happen again. Frequently there is absolute panic . . ." Ninety percent of the child-victims of parental kidnapping require psychotherapy, often for years following their return. As the parent of one of these children says, "We're never done with this. We never will be."

Out of Harm's Way:
Protecting Your Children from Parental Conflict

Children can continue to grow and thrive even through a divorce if their parents insulate them from intense or prolonged hostilities. Parents who accomplish this share some important qualities:

1. They make it clear that they value their child's relationship and time both with them *and* with the other parent.
2. They work out a fair and practical timesharing schedule, either temporary or long-term, as soon as possible.
3. Once that agreement is reached, they make every effort to live up to its terms.
4. They tell each other in advance about necessary changes in plans.
5. They are reasonably flexible in "trading off" to accommodate the other parent's needs.
6. They prepare the child, in a positive way, for each upcoming stay with the other parent.
7. The *do not* conduct adult business when they meet to transfer the child.
8. They refrain from using the child as a confidant, messenger, bill collector, or spy.
9. They listen caringly but encourage their child to work out problems with the other parent directly.
10. They work on their problems with each other in private.

- Children who are involved in parental conflict, even without physical violence or child stealing, are at increased risk for adjustment problems. A team of New York pediatricians studied 133 children from 87 families. Their most significant finding was that the more parental conflict the children experienced the worse their adaptation as young adults. Many children were able to get over the immediately hurtful effects of divorce, but found continuing parental conflict harder to deal with. These children "often felt caught in the middle in the tensions and turmoil caused by parental discord," and were unable to find an effective way of coping. One nine-year-old boy spoke for every child caught in parental conflict. "I feel like a knot," he told me. "I can't get undone because both of my parents keep pulling on me and it just gets tighter and tighter."

Children win when their parents find ways to maintain their own personal well-being.

Being a parent is one of the most demanding jobs in the world. Above all, good parenting requires giving of oneself. Babies require enormous amounts of time, physical care, and affection. Toddlers require nonstop attention, patience, and training. School age children need a loving home, structure, and encouragement as they learn about themselves and the outside world. Teenagers' needs are equally intense and even more challenging because of their burgeoning desire for independence.

Most parents can and do meet their children's needs. However, when a parent's own basic needs are not being met, parenting becomes far more difficult, sometimes impossible. A parent who is emotionally disabled may be unable to give his or her children what they need.

Debbie was the mother of three children under ten. Her world was shattered when her husband left without warning, taking the children with him. For two terrifying weeks she tried to find out where he was through family, friends, and eventually the police. When she finally heard from him, he directed her to fly to Chicago where she was allowed to see her children for a few minutes in a cafe, and where she learned her husband was now living with another woman.

Debbie eventually took this matter to court, where she was awarded temporary custody of the children despite her husband's charges that she was an unfit mother. The only home she could afford for her family was a tiny apartment with inadequate heating, up a long, dark flight of stairs, on a run-down street.

The enormity of her losses are clear. Her marriage ended abruptly without any clear warning signs. Her husband left her to live with another woman. She was forced to leave her family, her friends, and the community she had lived in for over a decade. She had been reduced from financial security and an adequate standard of living to subsistence level, dependent on welfare and sporadic support from her husband. Without preparation, emotional support, or money, she had to hire a lawyer, appear and testify in court, and defend her parenting ability against a barrage of charges.

Is it any surprise that Debbie was impaired as a parent? Confused, bewildered, frightened, and depressed, she needed much more support than was available to her. How could she be expected to listen to the children, calm their fears, create a secure new home for them, and meet their intensified needs during such a desperate time for herself?

Of course the children were equally distraught. The youngest, a two-year-old, had become intensely hyperactive. He was a nonstop blur of motion, climbing on and falling off everything in sight. Five minutes in the same room with him would have exhausted any parent. The middle child, a girl of five, had regressed. Whining and babyish, she demanded to be held or talked to constantly. At the slightest hint of frustration, she launched into a full-fledged tantrum. The oldest child was just angry. His sullen face made it clear that he was determined to make anyone and everyone as miserable as he felt.

Although what Debbie and her children went through is an extreme, most of the parents who separate and divorce suffer significant emotional upset and do become impaired as parents to some degree. The levels of anxiety, depression, and anger that most parents experience as a marriage comes apart are toxic to children. Research shows that disrupted or diminished parenting by one or both parents is a major cause of the dismayingly high incidence of depression in children of divorce.

Parents who find ways of managing these destructive emotions are more able to continue to care for their children. Those parents who maintain their personal support systems—meaningful daily activities, friends, family, home, and standard of living—are also better able to meet their children's needs during divorce.

How Parents Can Win

Parents win when they move through the stages of divorce successfully (see Appendix IV). They win when they handle the stresses and problems of separation and divorce as adults, working to transform conflict into cooperation. They win when they utilize their feelings, energy, and intelligence to solve custody, contact, and financial problems efficiently and fairly. They win when they take care of themselves in order to be able to take care of their children. They win when they are able to separate emotionally rather than continuing to torture themselves and their spouses. They win when they work towards a meaningful, independent life for themselves, and grant the same to their ex-spouse. They win when they work to improve their own relationship with their children rather than to destroy the relationship between the children and their other parent. They win when they break free from endless conflict and build a good new life for themselves and their children.

Getting There

The key to a solution that benefits both parents and their children is to focus on reaching a fair and realistic parenting agreement—a plan that defines and stabilizes the basics of life for parents and children—as quickly as possible. Michael Lentz, a family court mediator, summarizes his years of experience in one crucial statement: "The nuts and bolts aren't important—Mom and Dad agreeing is." Without parental agreement, no custody plan is likely to work well; with it, any reasonable schedule has a good chance of working.

Parents frequently bring children to me because the children are having significant adjustment problems following a divorce.

Most often the parents feel that their child's problems are caused by the "nuts and bolts," the details or structure of the child custody plan—too much time with the other parent, too complicated a schedule, too many differences between the parents' lifestyles. These parents often point to changes in the children before or after a stay with the other parent as proof of their views.

Many children do become unusually quiet, moody, provocative, or resistive at these transitions. Even more serious problems sometimes appear, such as increased rebelliousness at home or problems at school after a stay with the other parent. Children may be frustrated when they leave clothes, toys, or homework at the wrong house, or when a stay with mom or dad conflicts with another activity. However, it is rare to find a child with serious problems caused by such day-to-day factors. Some young children may be confused by a complex schedule, some teenagers may resent missed activities or time away from friends. But, when the day-to-day realities of a custody plan do cause problems, those problems almost always respond to commonsense solutions or just fade away as the children get used to their new schedules and surroundings.

In contrast, it is not unusual to find children with severe problems caused directly by their parents' inability to agree on custody or other issues. This idea is extremely difficult to communicate to parents. Mothers and fathers tend to look for simple, everyday explanations for their children's ups and downs. If Chris wakes up in a bad mood, it is because he stayed up too late the night before. If Karen is not getting her homework done, a parent's insisting that she finish it before watching any television should solve the problem.

When these practical approaches do not work, parents are at times, perhaps through counseling, able to see more subtle causes for a child's behavior. These causes almost always involve the parents. Perhaps Chris is waking up in a bad mood because, when he does, it is Dad who is called on to deal with him, a dad whom he seldom sees otherwise. Karen may be falling behind in school because she is afraid she cannot live up to her mother's high expectations or compete with her older brother.

Similarly, children are much more likely to be disturbed by ongoing battles between their parents, especially about custody, than by the demands of even a complicated custody plan. A child's security is undermined at a basic level when parental fighting makes a stable parenting plan impossible.

Patricia's mother hated Patricia's father. According to Mom, Patricia's father was a liar, a thief, and a cheat. By leaving her and eventually starting a new family, he had abandoned both of them. She was unable to say anything about him that was not poisoned with contempt, unable to allow Patricia to do anything involving him without throwing up a hundred obstacles.

Patricia's father hated her mother. According to him, Mom was a bitch, a crazy woman who was poisoning Patricia against him. Her coldness, anger, and demands had driven him away, and since he had left she had treated him as if he had been convicted of treason. If he spoke of her at all, it was in absolute rage at her latest provocation.

Is it any surprise that Patricia, a sensitive and knowing teenager, became seriously ill when it was time to see her father, and, after one of the rare visits, when it was time to return to her mother? "I hate both of them," she cried, "because of what they tell me about each other. If they loved me, they wouldn't act like that."

The best custody arrangement for your child is not necessarily the simplest or the one with the fewest changes or demands for the child. Of course it must be workable and realistic, but more important it must be one that both of you agree upon. Similarly, there is no single arrangement that is best for all separated or divorced families.

One couple I know maintains three households. The children continue to live in the old family home, while their parents alternate between that home and their own apartments. A bright, lively teenager, the daughter of a friend, has spent alternate weeks in her divorced parents' homes since she was two. Another teenager has lived with her mother during the school year, and with her father most weekends and two months every summer. The parents of a two-year-old went against the advice of friends and professionals. Their little boy spends alternate nights with each parent—and seems to be thriving. For the next two years, while a divorced woman finishes school, the children will live with their father, spending time with their mother on alternate weekends and during vacations. Once she is through with her training, they plan to reverse this schedule.

As you attempt to figure out what is best for you and your children, you are likely to be besieged by advice from others—your parents, friends, and "experts." Much of this advice, and much of what you may think you know about divorce, is based on false assumptions and dogmatic assertions. Much will be contradictory or simply wrong. Common sense tells us that

- Sole custody remains the best solution for some families some of the time.
- Joint or shared custody is the best solution for some divorcing families, some of the time.
- Flexible, loosely defined approaches work well for some parents, but rigid, highly structured plans work better for others.
- A custody arrangement that works when the children are small may need to be changed when they start school or enter their teens.
- A custody plan may need to be revised when a parent goes to work, remarries, or moves.
- Parents may have to experiment with several different arrangements before finding the one that works best for their children and themselves.

Beyond Winning and Losing

As you end your marriage and attempt to build a new life, it is vital to realize that your opponent is not your ex-spouse. Both of you, along with your children, face the same enemies—unchecked anger, corrosive fear, inadequate resources, uncertainty, despair. You will win or lose depending on what you do, on how well or poorly you accept and manage your own overwhelming feelings, on how well or poorly you handle the irrational and potentially destructive behavior that may be displayed by your ex-spouse, your friends, your family, your adviser, *and* yourself.

The winning formula, then, is a kind of applied common sense. Since your own hurt, angry, and vindictive feelings are part of the problem, it makes sense to recognize them, manage them, reduce them, and discharge them in harmless or useful ways. Because domination, dishonesty, and manipulation lead to resistance, distrust, and revenge, it makes sense to pursue your goals for yourself and your children with fairness, determination, and patience. Since the hostile exchange of blows, physical or emotional, hurts both parents and children, common sense suggests replacing battles with better ways of communicating and solving problems. Since the adversarial legal system can so easily become part of the problem, negotiation and mediation become constructive alternatives.

As Ralph Waldo Emerson wrote more than one hundred years ago, "Nothing astonishes men so much as common-sense and plain dealing." The more powerfully you insist on an outcome in which you, your children, and your ex-spouse all win, the more able you will be to use your own strength, knowledge, and feelings to cut through the tangles of divorce in order to transform a painful and conflict-ridden situation into a solution that really works for you and your children.

CHAPTER 3

Children and Divorce: Facts vs. Myths

"Nothing is so firmly believed as what we know the least."
—Michel Montaigne

Unfortunately for parents and children today, many myths pervade the area of divorce and child custody. You can test this for yourself by asking parents and mental health professionals for their opinions on the issues discussed in this chapter. You will almost certainly get at least two radically different opinions on each point. When you find people who seem certain of their views, ask them for their reasons. When I do this I rarely get an answer more convincing than, "Everyone knows that," or, "That's what happened to my friend," or, even worse, "How could you even think otherwise!"

When divorcing parents are imprisoned by inaccurate or misleading ideas, they often act in needlessly destructive ways. It would take a very brave mother, for example, to allow her two-year-old to spend substantial time with his father if all she had heard from counselors and other parents was the myth that her child would be terribly damaged by being separated from her for more than a few hours at a time. She might well view her ex-husband's insistence on such contact with his son as a sign of selfish disregard for the child, and feel forced to fight to protect her child. For this mother, learning that many young children can handle frequent overnights or even longer stays with a caring parent might free her from a needless battle or unnecessary worry and guilt.

In recent years many parents have explored new ways of parenting after divorce. Their experiences, along with careful research, have revealed helpful facts and challenged established myths.

Myth #1: Divorce Always Damages Children.

It is true that very few children react positively to their parents' separation. Many show signs of confusion, anger, anxiety, or depression for weeks or months after a parent leaves. Even years later many children still yearn for their original home and wish that their parents had not divorced.

Although few people, parents or professionals, would describe divorce as good for children, many parents carry an undue, often crippling load of guilt based on their conscious or unconscious belief that by divorcing they have irreparably damaged their children, now the unfortunate products of a "broken home." Friends and family members frequently add to this grim burden by blaming or by being angry, hurt, or overly protective toward the divorcing parents or their children. Perhaps the deadliest part of this myth lies buried in the phrase, "a broken home." The image this conjures up is a pathetic one—perhaps an otherwise pleasant, tree-lined suburban street with one home shattered by a bolt of lightning, the dazed mother and her children weeping on the sidewalk, father nowhere to be found.

Several excellent long-term studies show that children do go through a period of disturbance following divorce, that many children retain negative feelings about their parents' divorce, but that severe emotional or behavioral problems from the divorce can no longer be found after the passage of several years.

For example, two New York pediatricians, Stella Chess and Alexander Thomas, studied 133 children from early infancy. During the years of the study, the parents of 35 of these children divorced. When the children were in their late teens or early twenties they were rated in thirteen different life areas, including relations with family, school work, social functioning, expressiveness, drug use, and psychological and physical health. The results—there were no significant differences in adjustment between the young adults from the divorced and intact families. (In keeping with many other studies, these researchers found that high levels of parental *conflict* early in a child's life were associated with adjustment problems as adults.)

Fact: Less than one-third of American families fit the stereotype of a working father, a stay-at-home mother, and their children. According the U.S. census bureau, more than one-fifth of American children live in single-parent homes today; nearly half will do so for a substantial part of their lives. Fifty percent of married or divorced mothers with children under five are working, and an even higher percentage of those with older children. Nearly half of the married women with infants under the age of one are working. Current estimates indicate that by 1990 only 40 percent of the children born in the United States will live with both natural parents throughout their childhood.

Fact: American children today grow up in a wide variety of family structures, all of which are capable of producing healthy, well-adjusted adults. These family structures include the shrinking number of one-worker families headed by a married couple, the seven million homes headed by single parents, the rapidly increasing number of homes headed by unmarried singles or couples, the burgeoning number of blended families, and the millions of children now growing up in one of the many kinds of shared custody arrangements.

Although the many research studies that show relatively good outcomes for children of divorce are encouraging, many of us have seen for ourselves children who developed serious emotional, behavioral, or academic problems when their parents divorced. Many adults have lived through the divorce of their own parents and look back on those times with hurt, anger, or bitterness. How do these research studies explain the many children who are hurt by their parents' divorce?

One factor is time. Most children do react to the loss of the two-parent home they knew. Children frequently are angry at the parent who leaves the home, or at the parent they blame for the divorce. Children often regress, show signs of withdrawal, or become depressed in response to the unwanted changes of divorce. However, difficult and painful as these reactions are, most children manage to get back on their feet emotionally and behaviorally within one to two years of their parents' separation.

Another answer may be found in the work of Deborah Luepnitz, a psychologist at the Philadelphia Child Guidance Clinic. She carried out an in-depth study of ninety-one children and their families. Her findings showed that only continued parental conflict predicted poor adjustment in children of divorce. She came to view divorce as a family and personal crisis that could lead to lower *or higher* levels of functioning. Indeed, how often have we failed to notice the helpful, mature, self-assured, and independent children of divorce because we have assumed they could not exist?

Study after study has shown that the quality of what happens as parents grow apart, separate, and divorce determines how the children respond. Prolonged or intense parental hostility and conflict does hurt children. Loyalty conflicts can make children miserable. Loss of contact with a parent hurts children. So does the dramatic reduction in standard of living faced by many single mothers and their children, as does living in the chaotic world of a parent who has become embittered and depressed to the point of no longer being able to provide adequate care.

Fact: When these destructive factors are minimized, the children of divorce can no longer be distinguished from children in two-parent homes.

Myth #2: Children Need One Home.

In their book *Beyond the Best Interests of the Child*, published in 1973, Joseph Goldstein, Anna Freud, and Albert Solnit write, "Children have difficulty in relating positively to, profiting from, and maintaining the contact with two psychological parents who are not in positive contact with each other. Loyalty conflicts are common and normal under such conditions and may have devastating consequences by destroying the child's positive relationships to both parents." This influential book, which voiced the belief of many parents and mental-health professionals, advocated minimal contact between children and a non-custodial parent.

It is true that some divorced couples continue to fight so bitterly that their children cannot maintain a viable relationship with both parents. It is true that many spouses, frustrated by the limitations and ambiguities of the role of noncustodial parent, eventually drop out or drift away. I have seen a few children whose parents divorced when they were very young, and who hardly know another parent exists. I have also seen children who, trapped in a nightmarish world of parental hostility and violence, escape by rejecting one parent totally.

The key point is that children content with a relationship with only one parent are in the minority. The majority of children want desperately to maintain loving relationships with both parents. The overwhelming majority of children have two psychological parents, not one. What child, given the choice, would not want to continue to be loved, wanted, and cared for by both parents? Isn't it evident that an orderly transition from the shared parenting of marriage to shared parenting after divorce offers the children more continuity, not less? Research has helped to answer these questions.

Fact: A long-term study of sixty California families by child specialists Judith Wallerstein and Joan Kelly demonstrated that children adjust better to divorce when they continue to have stable and loving relationships with both parents.

When Dr. Leupnitz interviewed the children in her study three to four years after separation, she found that nearly all of the joint custody children were content with the arrangement. Far from being confused, they were able to give clear reasons for their preference. Most important, even the children of joint-custody families in which the parents continued to battle, although deploring their parents' fighting, wanted to continue to see both parents.

The Group for the Advancement of Psychiatry is a prestigious independent association of three hundred psychiatrists.

They addressed this issue in the definitive book *Divorce, Child Custody and the Family*. After reviewing existing research and consulting with experts in other professions, they concluded, "We find no evidence for the existence of a single psychological parent with whom the tie is critically more important than the rest of the network." Their recommendations are unequivocal:

> The court's determination should aim at providing the child with an ongoing relationship with as many members of his or her family of origin as possible. We are convinced that this is more helpful in the long run and less disruptive than a primary relationship with one parent and treating the non-custodial parent as though he or she were a visitor in the child's life.

Fact: These research findings are now reflected in the laws of many states, which make it public policy to assure minor children of frequent and continuing contact with both parents.

Myth #3: Children Must Be with Their Mothers.

Few issues create as much controversy as this one. Our evolution as a species has endowed us with powerful motivations and immense capacities to nurture our children. Whatever we have learned in our own subcultures and families, society dictates that the parental role, especially for women, is crucial. When we talk about where children belong we are talking about the parent-child relationship, one of the strongest bonds we ever experience, about women's and men's identities, and about broader issues of money, power, and sexual politics.

Fact: Children need to be wanted. Children need to be carried in the womb of a healthy, well-nourished, and secure mother. Children need to be born into a family system that has the financial and emotional resources to raise them. Children need to bond at a deep emotional level with one or more adults who, equally bonded, are motivated and enabled to go beyond their own egocentric needs to provide love, physical care, emotional nurturance, and guidance despite the frustrations and provocations of parenting. In a less-than-perfect world children need to have as many of these basic needs met as consistently as possible.

Despite recent social changes, mothers continue to do much more of the work of meeting their children's needs than do fathers, particularly during the early years. Relatively few fathers predominantly perform such basic caretaking tasks as nursing, diaper changing, bathing, toilet training, shopping for food and clothing, cooking, housecleaning, dealing with the school system, helping with homework, facilitating children's extracurricular activities, scheduling and getting children to dentists and doctors, caring for sick children, finding and monitoring babysitters, etc.

Mothers' greater involvement with childrearing continues despite our currently high divorce rate and legal and social changes making shared custody and father custody more frequent. Current estimates are that 90 percent of single-parent homes are headed by women, and that mothers continue to be granted custody of their children in close to 90 percent of divorces. Lenore Weitzman, researcher and author of *The Divorce Revolution*, predicts, "It seems unlikely that this pattern will change in any fundamental way in the near future because of the deeply ingrained social patterns that support women's greater investment in their children."

The generations of mothers who have done so much of the work of childrearing deserve our respect. However, respect and support for mothers should not be allowed to imprison women in the mothering role. When women are seen as the only competent parents, mothers who chose other involvements are vulnerable to crushing loads of criticism and guilt. Following divorce, choices other than sole mother custody appear unthinkable to many women, preventing them from exploring custody options that might work better for them and their children.

In their recent book *Who Will Take the Children: A New Custody Option for Divorcing Mothers and Fathers*, Susan Meyers and Joan Lakin, both of whom are therapists and non-custodial parents, argue that the most important criterion in choosing a primary parent is not sex but personality and motivation. "Who really wants the job?" they ask. "Who will be competent and committed?" They detail many reasons why a mother might choose to give up sole custody of her children. Like many divorced women, she may encounter severe economic hardships and decide not to inflict them on the children. She may seek to insulate the chidren from the impact of a period of personal and lifestyle instability that often follows divorce. She may desire to invest most of her time and energy into education or a career. She may recognize that the children's father is an equally good or better parent, or she may respect the father's strong desire to be the custodial parent. She may be supporting the children's preferences, or, particularly with older children, adjusting to increased difficulties with the children. She may be realizing her own need to develop apart from the demands and limitations of the primary parenting role.

Fact: Children clearly bond with both parents. Research using infants' protest at separation, greeting behavior on reunion, and comfort seeking when distressed have consistently shown that most children appear to be attached to both parents by eight months of age. Although normal children seek and derive comfort from either parent, infants of ten to eighteen months preferentially turn to their mothers when distressed. At the same time, children tend to direct more behaviors such as smiling and vocalizing to their fathers. From the age of two, boys tend to show strong preferences for their fathers on most measures of attachment, while girls, as a group, show no clear preference.

Many stereotypes about mothers and fathers exist. Mothers are thought to be more nurturing and caretaking, fathers more stimulating and playful. Mothers are seen as providing more emotional support and encouragement, while fathers take more action-oriented roles and are more likely to insist on adherence to strict sexual and social roles. However, careful studies show that mothers actually play with their children more than fathers do, although play takes up a larger proportion of the time spent by fathers with their children, and that both mothers and fathers strongly affect their children's sex-role and moral development.

Nationwide, about 10 percent of children are being raised

primarily by their fathers. The studies that have actually looked at how these male-parented families work have found that they have essentially the same strengths and the same problems as families headed by single mothers. Single fathers report the same feelings of inadequacy, the same frustrations at not having enough time with their children, and the same troubles juggling the demands of childrearing, work, and social life. Men with the responsibility of childrearing become increasingly aware of their children as individuals, and increasingly responsive to their emotional needs. How do the children do? Just about the same as children raised by single mothers.

Fact: Although it is better to have two well-functioning, nurturing, involved parents, research shows that, if such involvement cannot be, mothers and fathers are about equally able to handle the demanding job of being a single parent.

Myth #4: A Woman Who Does Not Keep Custody of Her Children Is Unloving or Unfit.

Noncustodial mothers are often seen as "deviant," as "unnatural," and as "failures," accused of abandoning their children even when they live nearby and continue to have close and frequent contact with them. In her 1982 book *Absentee Mothers*, Patricia Pascowicz notes that noncustodial mothers often lose relatives, friends, and even their jobs along with their primary parenting position. Many feel stigmatized and respond by isolating themselves or by keeping their parental status a secret. These rigid expectations do not exist only "out there," in family, friends, and the broader society; they are also rooted in the hearts and minds of millions of mothers, causing untold anguish and guilt.

Marie was a remarkable woman. She was intelligent, attractive, energetic, and had a wry sense of humor. She met her husband during their first year at medical school. When they decided to have children, they agreed that she would postpone her medical career until the children were "old enough." Her husband finished school and went on to a successful career. She raised the children with the same devotion and care she brought to everything she did. When the oldest was fifteen and the youngest six, she decided the children were now "old enough."

Her decision provoked intense reactions. Her husband, although initially supportive, became very angry as he realized what her full-time involvement with school really meant. He eventually filed for divorce and asked for sole custody. Her parents tried to be supportive of her, the children, and her husband, but secretly condemned her. Her mother particularly had no positive way of viewing another woman who, as she saw it, was abandoning her children. Most of her friends saw her in similar ways, either as bad—selfish, running away, rebellious— or as crazy. Even her therapist found it hard to see her as a growing person, not as an abandoning mother. Thus she had to deal not only with the challenges of being a reentry medical student, but with attacks, condemnation, and rejection by most of the people she had cared about and relied on throughout her life.

Marie ran headlong into the minefield of myths and misconceptions about women, motherhood, and divorce. Many people find it hard to imagine any good reasons or positive motivations for a mother devoting herself to anything except her children. Hence the negative choices perceived by her friends and family—she must be crazy or bad.

From Marie's point of view, she was acting for the best of reasons. Fairness dictated that, after a fifteen-year-long turn as primary parent, she should now be able to pursue the career interests that had always been as strong in her as in her husband. She loved her children and knew that their father could do an excellent job as the primary parent. She knew that, despite her full schedule, she would manage to give the children quality time. She was also aware that if she tried to be a full-time mother and a full-time student, she would make a mess of both.

Fact: As Phyllis Chesler reports in her book *Mothers on Trial*, most noncustodial mothers are quite ordinary. Most have been adequate primary parents for many years, and many continue to spend much of their time in traditional parenting activities. More than half continue to live close to their children, and almost all seek to maintain close relationships with them.

As long as the only legitimate roles for women are as wives

and mothers, then loss of custody, for whatever reasons, will be
seen as a sign of deviancy. As both men and women realize that
women can legitimately fill many roles—as wives or mothers,
as students, career women, artists, or workers—women will be
free to make caring and realistic choices about the custody of
their children without condemnation from society and guilt
from within themselves.

Myth #5: Young Children Can't Cope with the Separations and Changes Involved in Shared Parenting.

Marilyn and Charles separated when their daughter Kelly was
just fifteen months old.

"Right away, the first day," Marilyn explained, "we started
engineering the joint custody. Charles said that he wanted to be
with Kelly as much as he could. We both desperately loved
Kelly. Neither of us intended to use her as a weapon, and I think
that was the basis. From the day we separated we already had a
joint custody arrangement.

"It sounds really bizarre when I first tell people, so I just want
to warn you! It's the same as we have now—Kelly is with me
two nights a week, with Charles two nights a week, and she's
with each of us every other weekend."

"Did you know at the time," I asked, "from other parents or
from what you had heard, that most experts and most parents
would say that it could not work—that a schedule like that
would drive your child crazy?"

"Everyone did," Marilyn smiled, "everybody. But we both
knew we wanted to be there full time, and since we couldn't, we
were going to be there half time. From my perspective I'd rather
make a mistake on my own decision doing what I think is right,
than bow to someone else and find out it wasn't right anyway. It
wouldn't have been right for us."

"Did Kelly have problems—did she regress, or cling to either
of you, or have trouble sleeping, or get fussy because of all
those changes and separations?"

"Nope," Marilyn said flatly. "People are going to think that's
a big lie, but she took to it like a fish in water."

Contrast little Kelly's ability to move back and forth comfortably between two home environments for entire weekends with the recommendations of Dianne Skafte, a custody evaluator and mediator in Colorado. In her book *Child Custody Evaluations: A Practical Guide*, she writes, "As the child approaches three years old, entire days or evenings can profitably be spent away from home base, and overnight stays become appropriate. Entire weekends are often too long for children of this age." Clearly, Skafte's advice only perpetuates the myth that children cannot cope with the separations and movements involved in separate parenting.

Donna and Josh are the divorced parents of Casey, now two. They are both therapists and very aware of the assumption that children under three need one primary home with minimal disruption and change. They waited until Casey was eighteen months old before letting him spend weekends, including an overnight, with his father. To their surprise, this "didn't seem to bother him at all." He is now spending up to three nights in a row at his father's home, with no more adjustment problems than can be expected with any two-year-old.

Fact: Much of what is stated by experts on divorce and child custody is based on the assumption that a young child will have one home and one primary parent. This assumption makes visits or overnight stays with a noncustodial parent appear to be little more than disruptions to the child's routine and a source of insecurity. It seems very hard, even impossible, for these experts to imagine that a child can have two homes and two parents providing love, safety, and security.

I have seen many families in which the parents continued to fight about custody, where the hostility and tension were keenly felt each time the child went from one parent to the other. Under these warlike conditions, children of any age will avoid or resist transfers from home to home, or develop emotional or behavioral problems. Parents most often blame these problems on each other, or on the child's schedule. The real culprit—the parents' inability to get past their disagreements—usually goes unnoticed.

When parents agree that both will continue as "primary parents," and when each is able to make an adequate home for the children, then overnights can begin between twelve and eighteen months. Of course, each child is different. A child who clings or cries, or who shows significant anger or rejection when returned, may not be ready. Several months of frequent but shorter times for play and caretaking, perhaps at the home where the child is most comfortable, may be needed before that child is ready to spend nights with the other parent.

Many toddlers will adjust readily to two homes as long as they are not away from either parent for too long and they have had the chance to be loved and cared for consistently by both parents. Their need for stability is met more effectively by supporting close relationships with both parents even after divorce, than by rigid adherence to the idea that one home plus an uncomplicated schedule equals security.

Joan Kelly is a psychologist who has performed some of the best research concerning children of divorce. She writes:

> The child's need for stability in his daily life has been long identified as important in the ongoing development of the child. Within the intact family, stability implied stable care and routine, consistent caretakers, and some protection from erratic, capricious parenting. Yet, with divorce, the concept of stability underwent a transformation and became defined by many mental health professionals as one house, one toothbrush, and one primary parent. This *geographic definition* of stability took precedent in our thinking and decision making over the equally (if not more) important aspect of stability that is provided by a continuing relationship with a loving parent who no longer lives in the child's home.

Fact: For children of divorce, real stability can only be guaranteed by parents who agree to and abide by a reasonable and fair parenting plan.

These five myths prevent many parents from solving their

real problems. Believed as absolutes, they close off the very paths that can lead to successful new lives after divorce.

Equally limiting are the kinds of destructive assumptions parents often harbor about each other, assumptions that need to be examined and questioned very carefully to keep them from derailing the rebuilding process.

Assumption #1: "My Ex Must Be Crazy."

Separation and divorce create intense emotional strains, strains that often cause irrational behavior and a reevaluation of the entire history of a couple. The openness, intimacy, and vulnerability that were felt in the early years may now be seen as foolishness, impulsivity, and blindness. The same qualities that drew the couple together now come to be seen negatively—spontaneity becomes unreliability, warm emotionality reappears as lack of control, strength turns into domination, flexibility into weakness, and stability into dullness.

For perhaps half of divorcing parents, however, this reinterpretation of the past goes even farther. When feelings are exceptionally strong, when there has been deceit, betrayal, or angry explosions, when vulnerability makes accepting the fact of rejection and loss unbearable, it is all too easy to turn your image of your spouse upside down, to "discover" how evil or crazy he or she really is, really was all along.

San Francisco psychologists Janet Johnston, Linda Campbell, and Mary Tall identified this powerful process in many of the divorcing couples they studied, calling it "the negative reconstruction of spousal identity." They found that this destructive distortion of perception was a crucial turning point, often leading to bitter, protracted conflict.

These researchers and therapists point out that in the upheavals around separation, "desperate, unusual, and irrational behavior" is frequent, often as an attempt to understand or control what is happening, or to try to save the marriage. Behavior that is highly *atypical*—hysterical outbursts, suicide attempts, threats, physical struggles, child and possession snatching, flagrant promiscuity—comes to be seen as "the enduring character or personality of the ex-spouse." They write, "It follows that they can accuse each other of outrageous deeds (e.g., child molestation, neglect and abuse, maniacal violence, substance abuse) with little or no evidence."

Three kinds of couples appear particularly vulnerable. Some are couples who came together passionately and impulsively, only to find themselves equally unable to live with each other or apart from each other. For some, long-standing, destructive marital patterns continued, often more intensely, after separation. Still others are the victims of unacceptable shock and betrayal because of secret infidelity, sudden violence, or abandonment.

Shirley and Jack are the victims of this kind of perceptual change. They once were very much in love. The first eight years of their marriage were idyllic. Their friends saw them as a model couple. They were raising three delightful children. If they had been asked a year before their separation, they would have described each other as loving, caring, and devoted partners and parents.

Shirley, however, had a passionate affair with a dashing older man. Jack learned of this affair through a friend and felt terribly betrayed. He confronted her lover and threatened Shirley with divorce if she did not end the affair at once. She felt guilty and defensive; he became distant, suspicious, and developed a hair-trigger temper towards her. Twice their arguments led to physical fights. Following one of these, Shirley left with the children. Jack responded by following her to her parents' home and, when she refused to see him, breaking down the door. Shirley called the police.

When I first saw them, soon after this incident, each was convinced that the other was, and always had been, crazy and bad. Jack saw Shirley as "that lying bitch," a woman who had never loved him or the children, who had deceived and taken advantage of him from the beginning of their relationship. Shirley was equally convinced that Jack had always been cruel, threatening, and controlling. His violent nature had not surfaced before, she now felt, only because she had always done what he wanted—he certainly could not be trusted around her or the children.

Friends, family members, and even therapists and attorneys frequently contribute to, and sometimes cause, this kind of destructive distortion, either by blind one-sided support or by adding their own distortions, anger, or uncompromising advice to an already volatile situation.

As you go through the trauma of separation and divorce, remember that neither you nor your ex-spouse can be expected to act as maturely, sensibly, or wisely as you usually do. If you are lucky, you may be able to look back on your behavior during the first year or two of your separation with a rueful laugh. If you allow the confusion, hurt, and anger to control your actions and perceptions, they can easily cement you into a corner from which you can only see your ex-spouse as a bad or crazy person. Then you may never be able to separate emotionally, truly divorce yourself from your spouse, and rebuild your life.

Assumption #2: "My Ex Will Never Change."

This assumption is the mirror image of the above. Just as the emotional forces of divorce can make us think that the person we once loved has changed from someone worthy of our best into a monster, the same forces can convince us that there is no room or hope for improvement.

This conviction frequently emerges around the issue of a father's involvement with his children. Many women have told me, "He never did anything with the children. If he is given even part-time responsibility for then, he'll ignore them, he won't know what to do."

Research has shown, however, that little correlation exists between men's involvement with their children before and after divorce. Many men who were deeply involved with their children drift away after divorce, usually when they have been awarded little meaningful contact with the children. When they gain independent responsibility for the children, many men who were relatively uninvolved during the marriage become loving and responsive parents after divorce.

Trust is a precious and fragile thing. In the storm of divorce it is not surprising that both men and women complain that they can no longer trust their ex-partners. Their behavior before or during the separation has proved them to be unreliable, dishonest, erratic, or worse. "How can we work anything out," they ask, "when they've broken every promise they ever made?" Abigail Trafford, author of *Crazy Time: Surviving Divorce*, writes:

> There is nothing funny or easy about divorce. It is a savage emotional journey. . . . Most people go a little crazy. You are rarely prepared for the practical or emotional turmoil that lies ahead. You swing between euphoria, violent rage and depression. You may be promiscuous and drink too much; you may withdraw from people and not answer the phone. . . . No one told you it could be like this.

It is not surprising that in the midst of this turmoil most of us do and say things that are far from typical of us. Needs and directions change, many things are said or done in passion, promises are made and broken. The crucial point to remember is that this upheaval is not for all time. As Trafford writes, "In time, you discover that many people have gone through a divorce—and not only survived but flourished." For most, the drinking, the promiscuity, the withdrawal, the desperation come to an end. And we are changed, often for the better.

Refusing to communicate or attempt to work things out because you no longer trust your ex-spouse guarantees failure. Parents who come through this cataclysm successfully assume that trust can be re-earned and rebuilt. Common sense tells us that the only way to do this is to continue, however cautiously, with mutual problem solving.

Assumption #3: "We Will Never Be Able to Cooperate, Even about the Children."

Professionals and parents alike fall prey to this destructive assumption. Therapists, lawyers, and judges see divorcing parents fighting bitterly about support, pension plans, even household appliances, and, underneath that, fighting even more desperately about who is to blame for the breakup of the marriage. It is hard to imagine these same people communicating well enough to share the responsibilities of parenting.

Professionals often add to this problem through the mistaken belief that a cooperative relationship following divorce is sick—an indication that the couple never really separated. In a study of the attitudes of clergy, therapists, and lawyers toward divorce, psychologist Kenneth Kressel found that the majority of them considered friendly relations after divorce to be pathological.

In reality, it is those couples who continue to feud following divorce who are maintaining a pathological intimacy, not those who manage to maintain friendly or businesslike relationships.

Despite the crisis of divorce and the myth that continued hostility is the norm, many parents work out positive post-divorce relationships on their own. Constance Ahrons, a sociologist at the University of Southern California, has found that more than half of the divorced parents in her five-year study are "Cooperative Colleagues" or "Perfect Pals." They have varying amounts of interaction with each other, but are able to minimize potential conflicts and remain supportive of each other, particularly as parents. Interestingly, all of these parents still felt some anger over the divorce, but were able to talk it out or separate it from current parenting issues.

Most significantly, Ahrons found that even among those ex-spouses whose contacts remained full of conflict, almost all wished to be on better terms with each other. Even the angriest realized that an ideal parenting relationship would involve frequent and open communication with their ex-spouses. Clearly the motivation for a better relationship endures even when divorced parents are unable to get beyond their battles. Ahrons found that 64 percent of the women and more than half of the men had seen improvement in the relationship with their ex-spouse since the time of separation.

Over the years I have worked with many separated and divorced couples, many of whom had been battling for years. Some were not able to undo the damage that had been done and could not begin to work together. Most, however, were gradually able, step by step, to communicate, make and abide by tentative agreements, and begin to see the mutual benefits of trust and cooperation. Sometimes the most impressive fighters became the most successful problem solvers.

You and your children cannot live on myths. In the whirlpool of divorce, realities are the only rocks to cling to. One reality is that your children need two parents and, whatever their age, can readily adjust to having two homes. Most mothers are excellent parents, but fathers can be equally good, and are demonstrating this capability in large and growing numbers. Good mothers can and do share the custody of their children, even agreeing for the children to be in their father's custody when there are good reasons. Basically sound people do not become monsters. Constructive change is possible. Trust can be rebuilt. Don't let myths and destructive assumptions paralyze you with guilt or immobilize you with fear. You are the best judge of what you and your children need, and of what you and your ex-spouse can accomplish to nurture and protect them.

CHAPTER 4

The Legal System:
What to Expect

*I realized that the true function of a lawyer was to
unite parties riven asunder. The lesson was so indelibly burnt into
me that a large part of my time during the twenty years of my
practice as a lawyer was occupied in bringing about private
compromises of hundreds of cases.*
—Mahatma Ghandi

Before or soon after separating, most divorcing spouses seek legal advice. They hope to find an attorney who will inform them about their legal rights and responsibilities, help them to avoid potentially costly mistakes, protect their interests, and guide them through the legal steps of divorce.

Many divorcing parents do get caring and competent advice and guidance in all of these areas. Attorneys who are knowledgeable about family law *and* sensitive to the emotions and family dynamics of divorce help many parents reach a fair and livable outcome with as little animosity as possible. They help parents to utilize the no-fault divorce laws now in effect throughout the United States in order to restructure their families legally in a way that works as well as possible for both children and parents.

However, not every parent is so lucky. Many end up with lawyers who, despite glowing promises, only make matters worse. Sometimes this compounding of the problem is due to the lawyer's inexperience or lack of specialized knowledge.

Such unnecessary trouble can be avoided by selecting an experienced, well-trained attorney who specializes in family law. At times, however, the problem is not one of incompetence or lack of knowledge, but of competence and expertise that are misapplied. Like mercenary soldiers hired by a government, overly aggressive or litigious lawyers can block communication, derail constructive negotiations, and push people towards an all-out war.

Adversary Process: The Wrong Model

The American legal system is based on the adversary process. Lawyers are trained, paid, and expected to advocate their client's cause aggressively. In a criminal case, for example, the prosecutor's job is to present the most damning evidence possible, while the opposing attorney must attack this evidence and present an equally one-sided defense. The same is true in any area of law where there are competing interests. A successful lawyer is one who wins for his side at any cost.

When this deeply ingrained approach is applied to divorce, particularly when children are involved, it becomes a prescription for disaster. Although divorcing parents do have competing economic interests and may be intensely at odds emotionally, they share a fundamental need and desire to protect and nurture their children. Both parents suffer if they let the adversarial legal system damage their children. Such damage can happen directly, for example, when a child has to testify against a parent in court, or indirectly through months or years of stress, hostility, and loyalty conflicts. Both parents suffer if they allow their differences to be intensified by the legal system to the degree that they cripple or destroy either of them as parents. In addition, children have intense needs of their own during a divorce that the adversary process does not protect. When father has his lawyer fighting for his side and mother has her lawyer fighting for hers, who is there to protect the children?

Attorneys Who Help / Attorneys Who Hurt

Choosing the right attorney is one of the most important decisions you will make in the process of divorce. In my experience, an attorney can truly help only by going beyond the limited role as an advocate for only one side to represent the best interests of the children as well. Lawyers who zealously advance the interests of their client without regard for the needs of the children can do enormous harm.

One young mother I worked with was as poorly equipped for parenting as she had been for marriage. She lived an artistic, haphazard life. By the time her husband left her, he was absolutely furious with her. He won an initial custody decree and made it extremely hard for her to spend any time with their son. She was lucky enough to find and retain a lawyer who was a model of what a family attorney should be. When she was outraged, her lawyer calmed her down. When she was ready to go straight to court to try to prove that she was right and her ex-husband was wrong, her attorney counseled patience. When she was depressed and ready to run away, her attorney gave her hope. In effect she taught her how to be an exemplary parent and an effective negotiator. Her ex-husband, despite his anger, gradually had to realize that she had changed. They were eventually able to work out an excellent shared parenting plan. Their son, who had been fearful and confused while they were fighting, once again became the happy child they remembered.

In contrast, another couple I knew had been married for fourteen years. They were one of those families who were doing reasonably well until they divorced. Both parents worked, spent time with their children, and had many close friends. They were relatively mature and well-functioning people who simply grew apart.

Unfortunately for all of them, the mother chose an attorney who was a highly successful criminal lawyer. He handled her case as he would any other. He attacked the father's credibility and character. He built his case by seizing on and exaggerating the arguments and angry exchanges which they, like many couples, had gone through. To "protect" his client, he told her not to speak to her ex-husband. Proud of his bargaining prowess, he rejected reasonable offers from the ex-husband and his attorney, always supporting his client's growing feeling that things were not fair.

Predictably the father became more threatened and enraged. When I last heard from him, he had fired his first attorney, an excellent family law specialist, and hired a "bomber" whose approach and reputation matched those of his ex-wife's attorney. Equally predictably, pitting his new champion against his ex-wife's did not solve their problems. They continue to be in and out of court, spending tens of thousands of dollars to litigate minor points. The children have retreated from both parents, realizing that loving either of them openly means alienating the other. The enmity they have built up will take years to overcome, regardless of who wins or loses.

Just as I would not go to an internist for heart surgery, I would not go to a lawyer whose training and methods, however effective they may be in other areas, are not appropriate for work with families. It takes a special kind of lawyer to deal constructively with divorce and child-custody problems. Attorneys, however high-powered, who cannot see beyond the adversary system are dangerous. They see their job as proving one person right and the other wrong. They represent their clients blindly, inflating rather than softening their sense of injury, accepting their necessarily one-sided views as the whole truth, often exaggerating their feelings to try to gain an advantage. They may encourage spying on one's ex-spouse, directly or through the children. They may encourage a client to act provocatively in order to trap the other side into saying or doing something damaging. They may allow or even encourage a client to negotiate in bad faith or violate existing agreements. I have known of attorneys who encourage or winked at child stealing. One lawyer has even written a book in which he calls child stealing "the court of last resort," totally ignoring the evidence that the motivation behind most child-stealing is vengeance and rage, not concern for the child.

Some lawyers understand that family law is different. They listen to and represent their clients, but recognize that their clients want to protect their children as well as themselves. They act as effective advocates, making sure that the agreements that are reached are fair to their clients, but they also recognize that, in a family, the way in which a decision is reached is often as important as what the agreement says. They are firm in defending their clients against attack, but equally firm in counseling them against their own impulsive or self-defeating actions. They take the time to teach their client about the law, about the steps that will have to be taken, about the costs, the delays, the threatening and infuriating procedures they may have to go through, what they can expect if they go to court. They consistently remember and remind their clients of the children's best interests. They are sensitive to the human needs of their clients and their families. They are committed to negotiating agreements whenever possible rather than maneuvering towards judicially-imposed decisions.

Many parents are drawn to lawyers who strongly support their position, whatever it is. Remember that your own feelings and judgments are bound to be distorted to some extent, and that part of a good attorney's job is to help a client sort out what he or she really wants and needs from temporary, unrealistic, or destructive desires for victory, escape, or revenge. "What a parent really wants," an experienced attorney explains, "is not necessarily having the child or having it every other weekend, but something deeper—consistent, high-quality contact with the child, and freedom from the threat that the other spouse is somehow going to take the child away. If the attorney's motivation is to support that, it makes for a whole different approach."

Finding an Attorney

It usually takes a considerable amount of selective "shopping" to find the right attorney. Lawyers I have spoken to recommend asking other divorced or divorcing friends, your local bar association, and any attorneys you may know for the names of good family lawyers. Whenever possible, find out why the person you are talking to is making that recommendation. Some state bar associations recognize certified family law specialists. This certification, like membership in the American Academy of Matrimonial Lawyers, reflects specialized knowledge and experience, although neither indicates an attorney's approach. I recommend that both parents seek out attorney-mediators. They are usually resolution-oriented, knowledgeable about family law, and expert in dealing with the emotions and dynamics of divorce.

Interviewing Lawyers:
Ten Key Questions

Call three or more recommended lawyers and speak to them personally on the telephone. Ask the kinds of questions listed below.

1. Do you have any special certification or credentials in family law?
2. What percentage of your work is devoted to family law?
3. What percentage of your family law practice is devoted to child custody and visitation?
4. How many child custody cases have you handled?
5. How much trial experience do you have in family law?
6. What organizations do you belong to that are related to family law?
7. Are you trained or experienced in mediation?
8. When do you think it is appropriate for a custody case to go to trial?
9. What percentage of your child custody cases have gone to trial?
10. How do you usually proceed with a custody case?

After asking these questions, briefly outline your own situation and ask how the attorney would proceed. Evaluate their responses in terms of your own goals and needs. For example, you might not want a lawyer who takes every divorce to court, but you may also not want an attorney who is afraid to go to trial when it is needed. In evaluating training, experience, and credentials, one thing can substitute for another.

If possible, arrange to meet for a brief consultation with

several of the attorneys you liked the best. Be sure to find out in advance about the cost of that meeting and their fees for handling your divorce. Many attorneys require a substantial payment in advance in order to retain their services.

Remember, you are hiring someone to work for you. You have the right to ask questions and to expect thoughtful, specific answers. You need an attorney with whom you feel comfortable and whom you can trust. Beware of anyone who promises too much—there is a fine line between reassurance and false promises. Most lawyers are busy, but watch out for those who do not take the time to understand your unique situation and needs.

What to Watch Out For

"Lawyers are really good at hyping themselves," one attorney points out. "They are looking for business to a certain extent. So it's not a totally selfless, neutral person you are going to. Watch out for promises. If somebody says that something is or is not going to happen with any certainty, beware. In an initial phone call or even the first interview you can't be making predictions. You need to say, 'Here's what I think will happen.' Lawyers tend to make a lot of bold statements on which people rely. Then they have to work the client back from there over time. It's one thing to reassure, but there is a fine line sometimes between reassuring and misleading."

Watch out for an attorney who starts out from the position, "We're going to get you exactly what you want," without any thought about what makes sense in the overall situation, and especially without awareness of the children's interests.

Watch out for an attorney who gets you into a more extreme or rigid position. If you leave the office angrier and more frustrated than when you arrived, red flags should go up.

Beware of attorneys who respond to your questions with vague generalities. You have every right to know about a lawyer's beliefs; when those beliefs are put into action they will catalyze your situation towards a peaceful settlement or towards a custody war. "Ask for specifics," one attorney advises. "Ask what percentage of their custody cases have gone to trial. Ask when they think it's appropriate for a custody case to go to trial. Ask if they start with an adversarial posture or if they try to settle first." An attorney who consistently brushes your questions and concerns aside may well be giving you an indication of how you will be treated later on.

"But What If They . . ."

When one parent latches onto an aggressive, adversarial lawyer, the other parent often feels extreme pressure to find an equally litigious champion of their own. Attorneys I have spoken to agree that all parents need an attorney who believes them and who will act forcefully on their behalf. However, they also recognize that having two attorneys who are "out to get it all" is not the solution. I have seen the best outcomes in cases involving a highly-aggresive "bomber" when the other side had an attorney who did not work angrily, but persistently, calmly, and firmly.

You need to find an attorney who gives you the mixture of support, guidance, information, and even confrontation that works for you. In the passionate arena of divorce, I have come to value those attorneys who are willing to take the risk of refocusing their clients on the children's needs, and who are willing to confront their clients when needed. "I have had many clients fly off the handle," says an expert family-law attorney, "and I have to come back again and again to the children's needs, point out to them that there is nothing wrong with the other parent as a parent, it's just that they are so mad at them. I remind them again and again that how the other person behaves towards them is not necessarily the way that parent behaves towards the children."

Initial Advice

The impact of the legal system can begin with the standard advice an attorney gives in an initial interview. For example, you may be told to protect your interests by staying in the house even though this means that you and your children must continue to live in an atmosphere of poisonous hostility. You may be advised to strip bank accounts or seize assets. One attorney tells his clients to take one drawer from every dresser so that they cannot be sold.

This kind of advice may or may not protect your immediate interests, but it completely fails to take into account your children's need, and hence your own, for you and your ex-spouse to be able to trust each other, communicate, and cooperate in the future. If your angriest fantasies could come true, so that you would never have to deal with your spouse again, why not strip the accounts or take the drawers? But if your children's future depends on having two parents who are able to work things out at least to a degree, can you afford to take steps that will inevitably come across to your ex-spouse as unfair, hostile, or provocative? In contrast to giving such unhealthy advice, a truly expert family attorney might be able to negotiate a temporary custody agreement that would allow the parents to separate physically with minimal risk to their future custodial or property rights.

In my experience, you cannot expect your attorney to warn you in advance that your ex-spouse is likely to respond in kind to needlessly provocative or damaging actions. Just as surgeons may become inured to the pain they inflict, lawyers can lose touch with the effects their everyday methods have on ordinary people. Clearly you need to take your attorney's advice seriously, but you also need to make the final decisions each step of the way.

The Rules of the Game

One thing that your lawyer can and should do is inform you about the laws pertaining to custody, visitation, and support in your state. Each state's laws are different, and they are constantly being modified by new legislation and precedent-setting judicial decisions. The laws of each state define what custody options are legally recognized. They also may indicate, by legislation or through leading cases, preference for a particular option. For example, California law defines joint custody, advocates it as a matter of public policy, makes it the presumed choice if both parents agree to it, and the preferred choice even if only one parent requests it. A parent seeking joint custody in New York would have a different experience. New York, along with many other states, has not yet defined joint or shared custody through legislation, although courts can and do make shared custody awards. Significant cases and the preferences of individual judges will determine whether or not the court will ratify or even consider a joint custody plan proposed by both parents, will consider a joint custody request made by one parent but opposed by the other, or will prefer sole legal custody. Appendix III summarizes custody laws in the fifty states.

In addition to helping you to understand the statutes and case law that bear on your custody situation, your lawyer will also be able to guide you through the maze of forms and procedures that govern the progress of your case through the court system. Each jurisdiction has its own detailed rules of procedure that only a lawyer practicing in that area will know well.

Representing Yourself

Some people attempt to represent themselves in their divorce. There are books showing how to do this, some of which are listed in the bibliography. This endeavor may make sense for two highly motivated parents who are in agreement about almost all issues. However, if you and your ex-spouse do not agree on important issues, you are almost certainly better off with a competent attorney or mediator. It is common knowledge among attorneys, judges, and divorce counselors that the worst cases often involve a parent who is attempting to represent himself or herself.

Negotiating an Agreement

Many judges and lawyers recognize that divorcing parents are much more likely to abide by an agreement reached through negotiation than one imposed on them by a court. In the complex area of finances and in the sensitive area of parenting, negotiation often produces more equitable and realistic results than a court could impose. Some courts recognize this fact by insisting that parents and their attorneys "meet and confer" before going to trial. Most attorneys experienced in family law make every effort to negotiate rather than litigate.

Because their clients may say things that can later be used against them, attorneys often advise divorcing people not to talk to each other. This defensive tactic has the unfortunate effect of making it impossible for the parents to check out any misperceptions or solve any problems on their own. Even something as simple as arranging a child's birthday party may have to be done through the attorneys. Your lawyer can help you more by teaching you to communicate and negotiate more effectively than by cutting off communication between you and your ex-spouse.

Negotiations typically proceed in stages. You may be able to work out most aspects of a custody agreement through talks with your ex-spouse. Sometimes lawyers can clear the way to agreement by exploring an issue or advocating a position that is too emotionally loaded for the parents to discuss. The attorneys may answer legal questions and draw attention to areas you may not have considered. The end result is a document that is comprehensive and legally acceptable, as well as agreeable to you and your ex-spouse.

Whether the bulk of the negotiation takes place between the two parents directly, through their lawyers, or in joint "meet and confer" sessions, it can be the most effective and least costly way to resolve differences. When it comes to family issues, good attorneys consistently foster good communication.

Mediation: An Underused Alternative

Mediation occurs when two people sit down with a neutral facilitator to work toward agreement on specific issues. In family matters a good mediator performs two vital functions: keeping the discussion focused on key issues, values, and goals; and helping the participants deal constructively with their strong feelings. In many communities there are well-trained attorney-mediators, therapist-mediators, and mediation teams composed of attorneys and mental health professionals.

An attorney who mediates for a couple cannot ethically represent either one of the parties. Since the ex-spouses' interests may conflict, the attorney also cannot represent them as a couple. As a result, most mediators recommend that each parent should have his or her agreement reviewed by an independent attorney before it is signed. Although this procedure sounds complex and costly, mediation often turns out to be the least expensive option, financially and emotionally. If you are motivated to stay in control of the decision-making process, there is no substitute for negotiation or mediation.

Some courts provide or even mandate a free mediation service for divorcing couples. You can be sure that the court mediators have worked with hundreds of couples, have a very clear picture of what the court is likely to do, and can help you and your ex-spouse to cut through extraneous matters to get to the core issue of what is best for your child. Although the amount of time that a court mediator can devote to your family may be limited, you may well be able to reach an agreement through this service. Your attorney or the court can tell you if mediation is mandated or available where you live.

Mental Health Evaluation: Pros and Cons

At times specific issues come up where the opinion of an expert may make more sense than a negotiated agreement, or may be the only way to reach agreement. For example, one parent may feel that a child is ready to start first grade while the other is sure the child needs another preschool year. One parent may feel that the children could not tolerate the changes involved in a custody plan favored by the other. Just as financial issues can be clarified by an independent appraisal or expert advice, many divisive custody issues can be resolved by seeking the opinion of a neutral expert in the area of families and children.

In some cases where mediation and negotiation have failed to move a couple towards a resolution, the court or the parties may seek a broader evaluation of the entire family by a mental health expert. The aim of this kind of evaluation is to answer the question of what is in the best interests of the children. To do this the evaluator has to become familiar with the family and its history, assess the strengths and weaknesses of each parent, identify the specific needs of the children, and evaluate available custody and visitation options.

The advantage of this procedure is that it allows an independent professional to make an informed and thoughtful recommendation concerning the best way to restructure a divorcing family. The disadvantages include handing over decision-making power to an outside person, feelings of vulnerability from this kind of scrutiny, and costs in terms of time and money.

Even if you and your ex-spouse disagree strongly, you and your attorneys may be able to agree on a family evaluation of this kind. Particularly if the issues in your situation are relatively subtle, and hence difficult to bring out effectively in court, a mutually agreed-upon evaluation may clarify many questions and move your case towards settlement.

Parents and their attorneys sometimes seek one-sided mental health evaluations to support their position in a custody battle. In my experience these evaluations-for-hire typically make matters worse; they simply provide more fuel for the fire. A mental-health evaluator has little chance of helping a family unless the procedures are strictly fair. For this reason, an evaluator will want to be jointly chosen, court appointed if possible, and will spend equal time and effort to get to know and understand both parents as well as work closely with the children.

The Paper War

The opportunities for legal procedures to wreak havoc in your life multiply if the attorneys begin to position your case for litigation. In the highly charged atmosphere of a divorce, even something as simple as filling out a form can spark an explosion.

Recently an attorney called me for advice on how to deal with his client's ex-husband. The man was threatening to kill his ex-wife and the attorney. This desperate threat was provoked when the man was served with legal papers that not only sought to overturn a previously negotiated financial agreement, but also reopened every issue, financial and otherwise, that he thought had been settled. The attorney remarked, "Of course I asked for everything. I always do. I guess he didn't know it really didn't mean anything, so he panicked."

"Asking for everything" is a standard procedure, just a way of staking out a bargaining position. Everyone knows that, except for you, your ex-spouse, and the millions of other people who are at the receiving end of these legal maneuvers with your security and happiness at stake.

Part of staying in control of the legal process is to make sure that no paper with which you are not satisfied leaves your attorney's office. Many legal papers include declarations. These are sworn statements that muster up support for whatever decisions are sought from the court. They may include sections written by the attorney, by the client, or by a third person—for example, a neighbor, family member, or expert witness. When submitted to the court, they become part of the case file and may be read by the judge before deciding the case. Attorneys use them routinely to present a positive view of their clients and a negative view of the opposition.

Many lawyers do not hesitate to file a declaration alleging all kinds of wrongdoing by their client's ex-spouse, with little or no regard for accuracy. They assume, if they think about it at all, that their denunciations will be balanced by a similarly one-sided declaration from the other side. In the climate of mistrust and hostility created in part by the adversary process, this self-fulfilling prophecy is usually correct. What many lawyers become blind to is the effect of these papers on a divorcing parent: shock; the sickening feeling of having been betrayed, anger at having the worst moments of one's life taken out of context, exaggerated beyond recognition, and paraded as typical behavior in a sworn legal document. The end result is burning resentment or icy determination to defend oneself, to get even at all costs. In this escalating family war, nobody stops to ask if the very first shot was needed, if this costly battle had to take place at all.

Discovery

It is often necessary to obtain accurate information about financial or other matters. Lawyers do this through what they call "discovery." The court gives attorneys the power to issue subpeonas compelling a person to supply documents or appear in person to answer questions in a deposition. Attorneys can also require litigants to answer interrogatories—written lists of questions. The discovery process is a standard legal procedure guaranteeing that each side has the information needed to reach a fair decision.

However, if discovery is used thoughtlessly, aggressively, or punitively, it can produce extemely destructive results. We are accustomed to our privacy and freedom and value them highly. Most people experience these legal procedures as intrusive, coercive, and demeaning. Used sensibly as part of a legal problem-solving process, they may be tolerable. Misused, they become frustrating, frightening, and infuriating. I know several people who have lost their jobs as the result of depositions that were drawn out for days, many who will never be able to forget or forgive the overwhelming nastiness that this kind of interrogation conveyed, and still others, men and women, who simply describe the discovery process as having been raped.

"I Just Want My Day in Court"

Many divorcing people enter the legal system expecting to gain vindication and justice at the hands of a fair and wise judge. They hope that their day in court will set the record straight, will clear their name of the allegations made against them. Most end up disappointed. In many cases a divorcing couple never appears before a judge. Even in the relatively few cases that are decided in court, months or years of painful legal wrangling may precede the trial. Often the legal battle takes on a life of its own, with parents mortgaging their future and destroying their relations with each other and their children in order to win. Even the wisest judge may not be able to dispense fairness or justice. One judge explains, "I'm sorry, but that's the one area of law where I cannot be just. Justice says fairness to both sides. Child custody law says no—the standard is what is best for the child."

Whatever the outcome, going though a custody trial is a nightmare for most people. To "win," parents have to prove that they are the better parent. This endeavor usually means showing that the other parent is unfit. Since many custody cases today involve perfectly adequate parents, people whose parenting would never have been questioned except for the divorce, proof of unfitness must be manufactured. This undertaking means pumping the children for any information that might be used against the other parent, coaching them to tell the court one-sided stories, and, in the extreme, actively turning a child against the other parent. Children are used as spies in their parent's homes. At times, parents, with or without their attorney's approval, file false charges of physical or sexual abuse against each other. Housekeepers, babysitters, family members, neighbors, and friends may be pulled into the fray to testify about incidents that cast doubt on a parent, while doctors, psychologists, or other professionals may be used to provide support for one side or the other. By the time a custody case actually goes to trial, parents are often so angry and threatened that they are willing to attack each other without restraint. An experienced judge may be able to sort through the charges and countercharges to make reasonable orders about custody and visitation, but nobody, judge, lawyer, or doctor, is going to be able to heal the wounds that this kind of ordeal inflicts on what once was a family.

Parents are forced to use the legal system to help them decide the custody of their children. By its very nature, our adversarial system almost inevitably pushes them toward a more hostile stance. Any parent who does not want the legal system to make a bad situation worse must be in contol of the process from the start. The first step in gaining that control is to chose an attorney who understands that winning, really winning, in a custody situation does not mean putting a family through a legal meat grinder, but instead means mutual problem solving—a diligent, hard-nosed search for a solution in which everyone wins.

One parent told me that the legal system seemed like a wild horse that had run away with her family. Her advice, based on bitter experience, is to stay in control of the legal process from the first call shopping for an attorney to the day the final agreement is signed. If you do not, it can easily run away with you, your children, your money, and years of your life.

Yet a good family lawyer can support you when you need support, counsel you when you need advice, and confront you when you need confrontation. He or she can help keep communication lines open between the parents and between the attorneys, can encourage and enable parents to solve their own problems, can foster negotiation before litigation, and can help create a fair solution and family peace rather than one-sided victory. The sooner you find this kind of help, the better. The legal maze is complex, and a wrong choice can be disastrous. It is important to have a lawyer who knows the way.

CHAPTER 5

Everyone Can Win

Does the quality of a family's life after divorce come down to the toss of a coin? Constance Ahrons and Roy H. Rodgers in their Binuclear Family Research Project found that just about half of their families had good outcomes, evolving into "perfect pals" or "cooperative colleagues." Perhaps the other half, those who became "angry associates" or "fiery foes," were just not as lucky.

Although the odds may be fifty-fifty, the hundreds of divorcing couples with whom I have worked have convinced me that luck has little to do with it. The family catastrophes that make headlines and the more common miseries that so many divorced parents and their children endure are almost always the result of a long trail of misdirected actions and reactions, each one forcing a couple farther from their real needs and goals.

Good outcomes are not accidental either; they are always the result of many well-chosen steps guided by patience, restraint, persistence, and care. It is crucial to remember that at any point either parent can reverse a destructive spiral, can defuse the bomb that is being built, can start to make winning rather than losing choices. The following ten keys to handling divorce constructively can guide you in this effort.

Ten Keys to Handling Divorce Constructively
1. Take responsibility—"the buck stops here."
2. Be persistent—don't give up or give in.
3. Create a colleague, not an enemy.
4. Deal with your own feelings.
5. Deal with your ex's feelings.

6. Manage conflict through communication—"talk isn't cheap."
7. Manage conflict through action—"think before you act, then think again."
8. Find out what you and your ex *really* want.
9. Explore options—search for a win-win solution.
10. Resolve conflict through negotiation or mediation.

Take Responsibility

Each of us is ultimately responsible for our own problems and for their solutions. However, in our homes or offices, in our everyday roles, surrounded by familiar faces, it is so much easier to let responsibility slide away, let it hide behind someone else, anyone else. It is tempting to act like squabbling children, pointing fingers at each other, believing that our problems are largely caused by others, and, accordingly, blaming and looking to others for solutions.

How many times have you thought or said:

"I'm overweight because of her cooking."

"I only drink to be sociable."

"I got mad because she provoked me."

"I'm depressed because no one calls me."

"I got a ticket because the police officer had a quota to meet."

"I said that, but I didn't realize he would be hurt."

"I did it, but I didn't realize she would react that way."

The fact is that if I am overweight, it is because I take in more calories than my body needs. If I drink too much, it is because I choose to. I don't get mad because of someone else's acts, but as my habitual, chosen response. If nobody calls me, it is because I don't call others, or perhaps call on them too much. If I get a ticket, it is because I was driving too fast. As an adult, I am responsible for the predictable impact of my words and behavior on others. Of course, some problems are not of our own making; they arrive at out doorsteps without an invitation. However, the central, undeniable fact remains that whatever its source, the only way to solve a problem is to take responsibility for it.

Nor does this suggest that other people are not part of the

problem—many of our most painful and difficult dilemmas involve others. Nevertheless, the solution, the power to act, does not lie with someone else. At every moment, you have the reins in your hands. You can choose to gallop headlong into battle or run away. Or, you can stop, look around, and begin to choose your next steps as if your life depended on them.

Be Persistent—Don't Give Up or Give In

Jim Gumina is a terrific therapist and teacher. His way of working with people is unique—warm yet confrontive, persistent and goal directed, but full of surprises. I remember asking him for advice about a fourteen-year-old boy with whom I was working. Chad had been diagnosed as schizophrenic. Several doctors had told his parents to expect a lifetime of severe problems. I had been doing intensive psychotherapy with Chad and felt that the diagnosis was wrong, that he had the strength to recover. However, progress was painfully slow, and I asked Dr. Gumina if he thought I should end Chad's therapy. Jim, as he liked to do, leaned forward until his big, round face was inches from mine. "Bob," he said slowly, "failure is only determined by the point at which you decide to give up." As one father replied when I asked him what he would tell other divorcing parents, "No matter how bad it seems, it will get better. Remember that, and don't give up."

Giving in means accepting a less-than-adequate solution for the sake of escaping from conflict. For a mother, it might mean allowing her children to spend too much time with a father she knows is abusive in order to get enough financial support to live on, or accepting too little support in order to be relieved of the threat of losing custody. For a father, it might mean accepting ongoing abuse as the price for seeing his children, paying more than he can afford in order to "keep the peace," or leaving the children with a truly inadequate mother rather than facing her threats. The only conclusion worth working and negotiating for is the one that is best for all concerned, a solution that is realistic, workable, and fair. Neither giving up nor giving in can get you there.

Create a Colleague, Not an Enemy

We create enemies in our own minds by the force of our own hatred and fear. We give them power by the strength of our reactions to them, turn them into giants by our feelings of powerlessness. We teach them by the examples of our withdrawal and our attacks, and we hone their skills in our duels with them.

In working to untangle the conflicted intimacy of a failing marriage, anger and hurt are inevitable. Like a rocket fighting to break free of the earth's gravity, every inch of emotional distance that is gained has a cost—lost dreams, lost security, the loss of love, the loss of a valued and shared past. We turn someone we once loved into an enemy by striking out rather than dealing with our own pain, by refusing to accept our own share of the responsibility, by attacking to create company for our own misery.

Many people, including some in the helping professions, think that the only way to separate is by becoming enemies. This is false. Enemies are not separated at all; if anything they are more intimate than ever. Julie, a woman whose ex-husband kidnapped their daughter, described the three years it took her to find them. "He found this way to stay in my life all the time. He couldn't control me in the marriage, he couldn't hold me with money, so he held on to me through our daughter. For three years there wasn't one minute when I wasn't thinking about him."

Separation is not gained when lovers become enemies; it is achieved when people who once were intimate develop into separate individuals who can share the parenting of their children in a businesslike way. Think of someone you have known and worked with for a long time—someone with whom you are on cordial, businesslike terms, someone to whom you might send a greeting card once a year, with whom you can work things out sensibly and efficiently on the phone or on the job. If you can keep that picture in mind as the goal in your separation, you will save yourself and your children a lot of grief.

One trick seems to be not to act on impulse. Our instincts to attack and defend just do not work in the delicate and dangerous surgery of separation. Sandra, a woman whose shared parenting arrangement has given both her and her ex-husband eight years of stability and produced two spunky, self-confident teenagers, told me what it took in the early months of separation.

"I would say, when in doubt, don't say anything. Don't do anything impulsive. Anything, I mean, even deciding to go shopping! If it's from an impulse, don't do it, at least for the first year or so. Because I don't think you're rational. There are so many stresses that it just . . . it paid off for me to wait. If you're tempted, give yourself a week, and then if you still feel that way . . . if you still want to say that after a week, at least you'll have run it through your mind enough that it will come out in a rational fashion rather than angry.

Deal with Your Own Feelings

In divorcing, your own feelings can be your worst enemy. Your ex-spouse may hate you, your children may be hard to manage, and you may be struggling to find a job after years of full-time parenting. These problems are all severe, but they are survivable. They can all be conquered, if you start by managing your own reactions and feelings. I do not mean to imply that you should deny your feelings, pretending to be happy when you are crying inside, pretending to be pleased when you are seething with anger. I mean that you should give yourself permission to feel and respect your own emotions while finding ways to express or use them appropriately.

You have just found out that your ex-wife has registered your children in a private school without any discussion with you. Your impulse is to go straight to her house and tell her off, make her feel as badly as you did when you learned of this. You can act on your impulse, but only at the cost of adding more anger to the atmosphere in which all of you are living. Or, you can follow

Sandra's advice and mull it over for a week. Whatever you decide to do, you will no longer be acting out of rage, but out of the strength of knowing what you really want to accomplish.

Initially, especially if you have been seeking separation for a long time, you may feel relieved, even euphoric. If it is the other way around, however, and you do not want the divorce, are not prepared for what is happening, you may feel disbelief—it often takes a long time for understanding to penetrate all the way to your bones, longer still for acceptance. Once the impact of all that you have lost, all that is over, all that can never be, all that you now have to face alone, really hits you, you may experience an emotional crash. It may be sudden, an intensity of depression you've never felt before, or gradual, a flattening out of your feelings, a loss of pleasure, a lack of desire to do anything—a week, a month, or a year that you will not be able to look back at without shuddering. And with depression often comes fear—fear that you might not make it, that you will be overwhelmed by what you have to face.

Your anger can be a friend or an enemy. It can cut through your depression, give you the determination to get through. If it is directed against your children, it can do untold damage. I know too many children who came to hate their parents during the corrosive time following separation. If you lash out at your ex-spouse—and after all, who could be easier to blame—the two of you may never be able to escape the vicious circle of provocation and revenge.

My recommendations are simple, but putting them into practice is hard. Recognize your feelings. Keep a private journal of what you are going through, of what and how you are feeling day by day. Look into your feelings—underneath the blame and anger, is there fear and loneliness, a pressure to deny your own sense of failure and guilt? Somewhere within your depression is there a new version of you waiting to be born? Talk about what you are living through—not to everyone and not just anyone, but to those who have, as columnist Anna Quindlen puts it, "the ability to finish my sentences for me when I am sobbing." And if you cannot find friends like that, or bring yourself to let them know you at your most ragged times, then seek professional counseling.

Deal with Your Ex's Feelings

The first step in dealing constructively with your ex-spouse's strong feelings is to stop reacting to them—to disconnect the buttons and levers that have manipulated you throughout your relationship. Before you can begin to have a meaningful impact on someone else's feelings and behavior, you need to gain control of your own.

I saw a good example of this at a hotel recently. A guest was extremely angry at having been given a room that had not been cleaned. Confronting the unfortunate clerk, he loudly criticized every aspect of the hotel from management to decor. The clerk listened attentively. Finally, the man snarled, "And I have never had to deal with ruder help than you!" My respect for the clerk went up dramatically when he looked the enraged guest in the eye and replied calmly, "Thank you for that information. Would you like a different room or can I refer you to another hotel?" He was a professional, able to bring this ugly scene to a close by resolutely focusing on the business at hand.

Of course, it is much harder not to react when your ex-spouse is the person pushing your buttons, when he or she knows exactly where you are most vulnerable, when he or she threatens your financial security or your relationship with your children. It is hard, but not impossible. Parents who have taken this first step report that nothing gave them more hope, nothing did more to make them feel in control of themselves and their situation, than refusing to be provoked, holding fast to their goal instead.

The second step is listening—not just holding the telephone a foot from your ear and occasionally mumbling "uh huh," but actively seeking to understand what your former spouse is thinking, feeling, and trying to say. Psychologists are known and sometimes ridiculed for this kind of "active listening," which, in its simplest form, involves reflecting back not the words, but the essence of what has just been said. Sentences that reflect what we believe another person is feeling often start with the word "you." We do this because it works. Surprisingly, it works even when the other person is on guard against it. (Why be on guard against being understood?) In a first meeting with a college professor who had come to see me, he made his feelings about such techniques very clear.

"I've read all the books, and I know all those techniques. I'm going to be furious with you if you do any of that active listening."

"I see," I reflected, "you really don't want me to use any of those techniques on you!"

Pleased at being so clearly understood, the professor continued with his therapy session.

It is difficult to listen when you are the target of hostility, mistrust, or threats. It takes a great deal of self-control. At the same time, this simple technique is extremely powerful because it conveys to your ex-spouse the rare experience of really being heard. And, to the extent that you are really listening, you may begin to understand that your ex-spouse really has a legitimate point of view, that real needs underlie his or her words. Achieving that empathy is a crucial step towards resolving your conflicts.

The first step, then, is not to react with inappropriate emotions. The second step is to listen. The third step is to communicate your needs and ideas effectively.

Manage Conflict through Communication— "Talk Isn't Cheap"

Two things are vital in effective communication—what you say *and* how you say it. When we say one thing with our words and something else with our tone of voice, posture, or facial expression, people find it confusing, mystifying, and often maddening. When you say the same thing verbally and nonverbally, your communication becomes less provocative and far more effective.

Compare the impact of these statements:

"I'm angry because I couldn't pay the rent on time," rather than "You unreliable jerk, why can't you ever pay on time."

"It's vital to me to make my own decisions," rather than "Won't you ever stop trying to tell me how to run my life."

"I'm very worried by Kevin's confusion," rather than "You brainwashing bitch, if you keep badmouthing me to Kevin, I'll make sure you never see him again!"

Psychologist Thomas Gordon popularized the concepts of "I-messages" and "You-messages." He called them "I-messages" because the owning of responsibility usually results in a message that starts with "I." "You-messages" were the most direct way to convey listening and empathy. I used to teach people to use these ideas as a technique. The result was predictable—statements like, "I think you are a bastard," or "I feel that you are to blame for all of our problems." Once people understand the power of truly taking responsibility and the benefits of an objective statement rather than a personal attack, "I-messages" and "You-messages" come naturally.

A related skill is based on respect, on the assumption that if you can communicate a clear picture of the problem, the person to whom you are speaking will be far more willing to help solve it than if you diminish them by handing them, or demanding, your solution. Which statement would be more likely to encourage you to cooperate?

"I've been asked to go on a business trip next weekend," or "You'll have to keep the kids next weekend."

"Marty's teacher says he's getting teased about his teeth," or "When are you going to cough up the money for the orthodontist?"

In recent years thousands of parents, teachers, and executives have been taught effective communication through taking responsibility, listening actively, conveying respect, using "you-messages" and "I-messages," describing the problem, not the solution. Inevitably they raise two objections—"It's unnatural" and "It's too hard." Gaining enough self-control to begin to use these approaches is hard, and any new skill feels unnatural at first. But which is harder—mastering some new skills for effective communication, or trying to solve your problems with habitual ways of thinking and communicating that have themselves become part of the problem?

Manage Conflict through Action—"Think before You Act, Then Think Again."

Warring parents can be very creative at finding ways to keep the conflict pot full and boiling. Parents who are determined to resolve their custody conflicts constructively need to be equally creative at building respect, cooperation, and trust. Those who are most successful appear to base much of what they do on some of the following ideas.

1. They work hard to get beyond their own hurt, fear, and anger. They start rebuilding their own lives as quickly and as well as possible.
2. They accept their fair share of the responsibility for the breakup of their marriage and for their current problems—and say so.
3. They speak as positively as possible about their ex-spouses, particularly to or in front of their children. They don't deny their negative feelings, but they express them privately to people who can be trusted to help.
4. They really believe that the children need two parents, and they act accordingly. They plan their activities to facilitate the children's contact with the other parent. They go out of their way not to change or cancel a scheduled stay. They encourage the children to spend and enjoy time with the other parent.
5. They recognize that parental problems need to be solved between themselves. They make every effort to protect the children from adult issues and arguments.
6. They take time and trouble to share important decisions concerning the children. Even when they make an independent decision, if it affects the children or the other parent, they give the other parent as much advance notice as possible.
7. They realize that nobody is going to replace the other

parent in the children's hearts. They do not allow a new mate to be seen as replacing the other parent.

8. They make the children's stays in the other home as easy as possible, allowing clothes, toys, bicycles, etc., to move from home to home to meet the children's needs, not their own. They pick the children up and drop them off on time.

9. They recognize that transfers from home to home may cause temporary upsets; they make no more of those upsets than the hundreds of others that come and go.

10. They do their own communicating with the other parent. They never use the children as messengers or spies.

11. They facilitate the children's communication with the other parent. Phone calls are answered and returned. The children's privacy is respected. Mail and gifts are delivered.

12. Recognizing that financial security is vital, they make every effort to live up to their financial obligations. They make sure that support checks arrive consistently and on time.

13. They schedule private times for adult problem solving and decision making. They refuse to argue in front of the children.

14. When the children complain about the other parent, they listen carefully, but encourage the children to work it out with that parent. If a serious problem persists, they use all their skills to find a solution with the other parent.

15. They bring new partners into their own and their children's lives slowly and cautiously.

16. They make every effort to be on good terms with their ex-spouse's new mate.

17. They make special efforts to make sure that both parents get to share birthdays and holidays with the children.

18. They place a very high value on resolving their own disputes. Communication and problem solving come first.

19. Valuing fairness, cooperation, and resolution, they know when to stop. They realize that a fair and workable, even if less-than-perfect, resolution may be far better than continued conflict and uncertainty.

20. They tell and show their children that they are loved.

Find Out What You and Your Ex *Really* Want

I was lucky enough to observe Gary Friedman, a masterful attorney-mediator, working with a couple. The scene itself was dramatic—for close to an hour the couple had been fighting over issues that seemed insoluble, in front of an audience of twenty lawyers and therapists involved in a training program. In the intensity of their feelings, the divorcing parents had forgotten the audience; they were aware only of the impact of dealing with each other face-to-face. The quality of Gary's attention and his insistence on fairness made it safe for them to deal with their own feelings and with each other. His penetrating questions and ability to clarify things kept each of them moving closer to their own deepest values.

After negotiating about spousal support and division of financial assets, they finally started to talk about custody.

"I'm going for full custody of Danny." Joe practically threw the words at Phyllis.

"You goddamn bastard," she shot back.

"Phyllis," Gary said very quietly, "tell Joe what you're feeling."

It took Phyllis a minute to put some of her feelings into words. "I'm terribly angry at him for what he's doing. And I'm scared, scared for Danny and scared for me."

"Is there something Joe needs to understand that he's missing, something about your relationship with Danny?"

Gary's question caught her by surprise. She looked at Joe, studied his face, struggling to see him, to discover what was lacking in his understanding of her that would allow him to say what he had.

"My relationship with Danny? Oh. I see. He's so mad at me that he's wiping out what Danny means to me. He isn't counting Danny and me at all. That's what's so crazy, like he can't see us, he could just run right over us."

"Don't you understand that I'm frightened too?" Joe broke in.

"Of what?" Gary asked.

"Of losing Danny." There was a long, tense silence. "And

I'm frightened of losing control, of getting so mad that I really hurt someone."

Again Gary spoke slowly and quietly. "Do you know where all that anger is coming from?"

"I'm frustrated because she's *got* Danny."

"What does that mean?"

"That he lives in the house with her. It's like she's swallowed him up; I can't reach him."

"Do you know what you're afraid of?"

Joe groped in the air in front of him, then found some words. "It's like a hole, like a vacuum where Danny and Phyllis used to be. And I reach out for Danny and he's not there."

"When Danny is there, when you're holding him, what do you want to happen to him?"

"Nothing bad, ever." Joe choked the words out, brushing at the corner of his eye, "Just what's good for him."

"And what is that?"

Joe closed his eyes and folded his arms across his chest. He looked like he was holding Danny on his lap. "He needs me, that's for sure, but he needs Phyllis too. I know that."

The mediation continued, but in a very different tone. Danny was no longer a thing that Phyllis or Joe could own—he was a little boy whose needs they knew and felt more keenly than anyone else in the world. Joe's anger was no longer an alien force that threatened to spin out of control, but a comprehensive mixture of frustration and fear, still powerful, but his own. Phyllis' loving relationship with Danny had been seen, recognized, and valued by Joe. She did not need to be as frightened. Underneath the issues of money and the house and "custody" they had discovered their real feelings and values. Surprisingly, those feelings and values, like their love for Danny, were shared.

Within minutes Gary was able to ask, "Danny needs for you to be the best father, and for Phyllis to be the best mother. What would be a way to go about doing that?"

"I've got to find a place to live," Joe replied calmly, "a place where Danny can spend good time with me."

In the heat of a divorce it is easy to lose track of what you really want. Yet remembering it, finding it again, is the shortest road home. Not back to the home and family that is now gone, but on to a new home, a restructured family, a new life.

Working with an experienced mediator can help enormously. However, as Michael Nagler points out in *America Without Violence*, "The way to use mediation with potentially unlimited effectiveness . . . ? *Be your own mediator*. Personal style is the beginning, a style in which the mediator's detachment is . . . internalized. And the way to get upstream with this technique is by striving to use it constantly, not waiting until conflict and violence have erupted . . . an especially difficult task when we feel the configuration of conflict closing in. To listen unfailingly to an 'opponent's' point of view—indeed even to recognize that he or she *has* a point of view—is a powerful mechanism for resolution."

Explore Options—Search for a Win-Win Solution

In every negotiation, mediation, or attempt to solve a human problem, wide-ranging exploration of options is vital. Too often we take a position, defend it, and end up blinding ourselves to any other alternatives.

This happened with a vengeance in one family with which I worked. It was the father's second marriage. He had a fourteen-year-old son from the first marriage, a four-year-old boy from the second. Despite difficulties over the years, he and his first wife had maintained a particular pattern of visitation—the older boy stayed with him from after school on Tuesday through dinner on Wednesday, and every other weekend. Tony, the father, negotiated effectively with his second wife on issues of property and support. However, he adamantly insisted that his four-year-old stay with him at exactly the same times as his fourteen-year-old. He clung to this position as if were the last dry place in the flood. For several very good reasons, including the older boy's frequent tormenting and endangering of the younger, Tony's ex-wife felt such a plan was far from the best arrangement. She offered him more time with alternative schedules, but he could only see this one solution.

Eventually they went to court, where Tony continued to

refuse any other contact plan. After listening to both sides, the judge ordered a different, significantly better plan. Tony jumped up, denounced the judge for making a terrible decision, and refused to go along with it. The judge, who was noted for his care and restraint, eventually had to cite him for contempt and have him arrested.

In my experience, divorcing parents rarely explore all of the options open to them. Lawyers and accountants are fully aware of how important such exploration is regarding money matters. The complexities of each parent's changing financial resources and needs, coupled with tax laws, pensions, inheritance, creative financing, etc., means that there are often hundreds of constructive options. The best may never be perceived unless the parties and their attorneys communicate well enough to explore them thoroughly. The same is true regarding child custody. Most states now allow, and many encourage, joint legal custody and some form of shared parenting. With an increasing number of fathers being closely involved with their children from birth, and with an increasing number of two-career families, it makes sense to consider a wide variety of custody options and schedules. Many of these are discussed in Appendix II.

Negotiate: Not Hard /Not Soft

In their best-selling book *Getting to Yes*, Roger Fisher and William Ury of the Harvard Negotiation Project identify the keys to winning negotiation. They argue that negotiation needs to be judged by three questions. Does it reach a wise outcome? Is it efficient? Does it improve or at least not damage the relationship between the parties?

Fisher and Ury target the deficiencies of both hard and soft bargaining. Adamant positional bargaining, as Tony found out, often does not lead to a solution and is almost always damaging to the relationship between the parties. For parents, who have to share the rearing of a child for many years, such damage is often disastrous. Soft bargaining, yielding to threats and ultimatums, making concession after concession to reach agreement, is equally poor. The agreement reached is not likely to be wise or fair, and the soft bargainer's self-esteem and well-being are typical casualties. Particularly when your children are the silent partners to your negotiations with your ex-spouse, neither hard nor soft bargaining is the answer.

The alternative, which Fisher and Ury call *principled negotiation*, involves four basic points. They write:

Separate the people from the problem
Focus on interests, not positions
Generate a variety of possibilites before deciding what
to do
Insist that the result be based on some objective standard

The ideas discussed earlier in this chapter—taking responsibility, not giving in or giving up, conducting businesslike communication, coping with your own and your "adversary's" feelings, and managing conflict through appropriate communication and action—are effective means of "separating the problem from the people." Finding out what you really want, also discussed above, means focusing on deeper interests rather than on surface positions.

The central new idea that completes the principled negotiation approach is insisting on using an objective standard. The authors point out, "This does not mean insisting that the terms be based on the standard you select, but only that some fair standard such as market value, expert opinion, custom, or law determine the outcome." In negotiating about the custody of your child, this standard might mean agreeing to use the advice of an expert on children and families, or trying out several different custody plans and comparing them in terms of the children's responses to them.

In divorce there is no shortage of intensely-felt needs and powerful feelings. In situation after situation, we have seen how destructive this emotional energy can be when it is expressed in hostile ways. Principled negotiation is the ideal way to invest that power constructively. All of your strength, your deepest and strongest feelings, can be focused on making sure that your custody problems are solved through this fair, efficient non-damaging, and objective approach. If your goal is a fair and realistic resolution, and you are determined to get there through fair means, every drop of your strength, every ounce of your feelings, can be ploughed into that process.

Some couples can negotiate solutions to their financial and parenting problems with little outside help. Many are able to use principled negotiation within the structure of mediation. Attorneys who understand families negotiate successfully for parents and children in this way, in every state, every day.

At the end of one couple's negotiations, the father told me: "At the beginning we were both talking about who was right. Each of us was sure we knew what was best for Christie, our four-year-old daughter, but neither of us was really thinking about her at all. At this point I don't really care whose ideas are best or who has more clout—what counts is what works for Christie. And now that I can see how great she's doing, I realize that the things we compromised on so that we could agree weren't all that important."

CHAPTER 6

Separating

Separation marks the death of an old relationship and, if all goes well, the birth of a new one. Separation is a critical period, one of those times of heightened meaning and impact, as if everything were taking place under a spotlight. What happens during your separation may shape your life for years to come. Handled poorly, it may open wounds that never heal. Handled well, it sets the stage for good communication, respect for each other as parents, and for a real psychological separation.

Under the pressures of separation, it is very tempting to seek or accept quick solutions. You may be in a great deal of pain, your mood and feelings pushing the limits of your endurance. Anything that promises to reduce the pain seems attractive. In crisis, people often accept arrangements that are not fair, not workable, bad for themselves, or bad for their children. A devoted mother might accept an unlivable financial settlement to head off her husband's threat of a custody battle. A loving father may take on an unfair or crippling level of support payments to "buy" adequate contact with the children. I have seen many custody wars flare when a needy parent impulsively decided to take the children and flee "back home," perhaps thousands of miles away from the other parent.

During separation your goals need to be simple: to separate physically and begin to separate emotionally, to take care of your physical and emotional health, to stay close to and supportive of your children, to work out with your ex-partner livable temporary financial and custody arrangements. Although you may feel great pressure to finalize everything, to find permanent solutions, this is a time for surviving, for new beginnings, not for conclusions. Remember that you, your ex-spouse, and your children are probably at your worst right now; give yourselves time and emotional leeway. Permanent solutions will be easier to find later.

One Step towards Transformation

It is crucial to keep in mind that separation is one stage in a natural process that millions of families go through. For most couples, physical separation and the emotional "crazy time" that often follows, evolve, although not without pain and work, into new beginnings, and eventually into constructive new lives. As Constance Ahrons has shown, the final stage for many divorced families is a healthy new kind of family, one with two independent parents, two vital centers rather than one.

Nora and Mike are examples of this new kind of family. One year after a traumatic breakup, both are doing well. Nora is building her career, proud of how well she and her children are managing, and starting to enjoy life again, although her friends know how much more cautious and serious she has become. Even though her eyes sometimes fill with tears or flash with anger, she can talk openly about her ex-husband, his affair, his quick remarriage, and equally openly about her own part in the breakup of their marriage. A turning point for her was when Mike was able to admit that he had treated her badly before and during the separation. It also helped that his second wife has gone out of her way to make peace with Nora, a peace which Nora has gradually come to accept. The children spend about a third of their time at their father's home, and feel as comfortable and loved there as at their mother's. Everyone has begun to live again.

Stumbling Blocks

Julia, unlike Nora, has been unable to move through the stages of shock, denial, anger, and mourning, to move ahead with her life. A year after her husband's decision to leave, she continues to go over and over the same thoughts and feelings. "I don't understand," she still cries, "we loved each other so much. How could he do this to our children? To me? I still love him. I can't believe he won't come back someday." Julia continues to deny what is painfully obvious to everyone else. She has not yet faced the rage, the mourning, the letting go, and the rebuilding that Nora has put behind her.

Perhaps Julia was wounded more deeply than Nora. The deeper the wounds, the more massive the erosion of our stability, our security, our image of ourselves—the more desperate we become. In desperation we make frantic, uncharacteristic attempts to restore stability; inwardly we deny the reality of change, outwardly we may act recklessly to escape the pain or to try to force the pieces back together. In desperation, we often make things worse.

For the past five years, three psychologists at Children's Hospital in San Francisco, Janet Johnston, Linda Campbell, and Mary Tall, have studied and worked with divorced couples who have been unable to make a successful transition from marriage to stable separation. These couples, from every ethnic group and economic level, are trapped in intense disputes over the care and custody of their children. To unravel the knots that bind these unhappy couples, the psychologists asked one central question: "What is preventing the separated spouses from settling their disputes?" Their answers can serve as guideposts for all divorcing couples.

These researchers found that certain kinds of separations are very likely to lead to ceaseless conflict: "Being abandoned suddenly, being left after secret plotting and planning, being deserted for someone with whom one's spouse has been secretly having an affair, and being left after an explosive incident of violence are all separation modes that are typically traumatic; they involve inordinate degrees of humiliation, anger, defeat, guilt, fear, and betrayal." In addition, they found that long years of deeply troubled marriage, or extremely intense love-hate relationships, often set the stage for unresolvable disputes.

How do people react to these assaults on their psychological well-being? "Atypical behavior—hysterical outbursts, suicide attempts, ominous threats of murder, physical struggles, child and possession snatching, and flagrant promiscuity" were common. These were seen as "an attempt to restore the normative order of the marriage."

Irrational as it may seem, such behavior makes solid psychological sense. If the breakup is too threatening, if accepting that reality means accepting some deeply dreaded, unbearable conclusion—I am not lovable, I am not valuable, I can't control what I have to control to survive, I can't make it—then almost any action seems justified to put things back together. If hysterical pleading does not work, maybe threats will do the job. If threats do not put the shattered pieces back together, perhaps illness, collapse, or a suicide attempt will. Or, even more dangerously, "If I hurt this much, so will you." That kind of thinking leads to verbal abuse, threats, assaults, and, in the worst situations, to child stealing or even murder.

What can we learn from these couples, and from those who weather the divorce transition well, who are able to go on to live independent, happy lives?

Taking Care of Yourself Emotionally

Part of the lesson is to wait. Go slowly. Be patient with yourself. Be willing to suffer the long, gut-wrenching arguments, the longer silences, the widening distances and the painful attempts to restore intimacy, the unavoidable pain of working through your separation. Do not panic when depression sets in, when shock and denial slip into a numbness that feels like it may last forever. Do not be surprised when that numbness is pushed aside by sorrow and rage. Do not jump at the first hope for escape. Accept rather than fight what you are going through. As Mel Krantzler writes in his book *Creative Divorce*:

> Whatever the variations in schedule or impact of mourning, the positive benefits are greatest and most lasting when you recognize and accept, rather than resist, your feelings. These can include anger, fear, anxiety, resentment, vulnerability, and guilt—side by side with equally strong urges to return to the past. Your feelings may have always

been bottled up inside you; now is the time to let them out and make positive use of them.

As a therapist I used to dread working with couples in which one member had already decided to leave and was trying to get the other to accept this reality. I was drained by the wrenching confrontation between one partner's implacable resolve to leave and the other's often desperate resistance. However, I have come to see that, painful as this work is, it can be tremendously helpful to a couple, can help them through the divorce impasse so that they can go on with their lives.

Affirmations

Taking care of ourselves in the midst of the separation crisis starts with two statements most of us find incredibly hard to make—and truly believe. The first: "I'm OK. My feelings, the changes I am going through are healthy, normal, and good. Through this pain I am growing, becoming more capable, more valuable, more worthy of being loved. However much I hurt, this is not death, but rebirth." The second: "I am responsible. I may not have created all of the problems, and I cannot control anyone else, but I accept responsibility for taking care of myself and for solving my own problems."

A Little Help from Your Friends

Research studies and common sense agree on one fact: people who have a network of support, caring friends, or family do far better during and after a crisis than those who do not. In ten years of working with troubled people, I have yet to find a person with nobody to turn to. I have, however, worked with many lonely people who would not reach out for the help they needed. Pride, fear of rejection, worry about asking for too much, or feelings of unworthiness may stand in the way of getting needed support.

Yet, if any one quality truly makes us human, it is our willingess to listen, to care, to help when someone needs us. No matter how isolated you feel, someone you know is there for you. Tell them what is happening to you; it does not make sense to carry this kind of burden, make decisions on which so much depends, on your own. Having at least one person with whom you can be honest is vital; benefiting from caring, thoughtful listening from more than one friend is even better.

There is no time when therapy or counseling can be of more help than during a crisis. Crisis times, however chaotic and frightening they may be, are times of great opportunity for change. Friends or family members, however caring and under-standing, may be so closely attuned to you that they are unable to give you one vital ingredient in this process—a change in perspective, a view through unprejudiced eyes, a new way of looking at what is happening. Through your friends, your thera-pist, or on your own, you may be able to find or put together a support group in your own community—parents going through the same process that you are. Few things could do more to help you during this period.

The friends and therapists who have helped me in times of crisis glow in my memory like beacons. I might have blundered through, sooner or later, on my own, but their unwavering support, their warmth and caring, their ability to show me a fuller vision than I was able to see, removed obstacles from my path, helped me to keep going. Why not give yourself this gift?

Taking Care of Yourself Physically

While caring for yourself emotionally involves reaching out to others, the equally important responsibility of caring for your-self physically falls to you. This is a time to treat yourself as well as you can. Make sure you eat well, even if depression robs you of your appetite or pushes you to gorge on sweets. Sleep well. A very important investment of whatever resources you have is to get away. Even an overnight at a friend's house, a twenty-four hour "vacation" from your day-to-day preoccupa-tions, can help you break out of the rut. Most people find that physical activity—the more intense the better—helps them to "blow off steam" and leaves them feeling better afterward.

Research has shown that learning new skills or improving old ones is one of the most powerful antidotes to depression. This is

an ideal time to take a class, attend workshops, join a self-help
or interest group. At the same time, increased involvement with
a long-familiar activity, with familiar sports or games, with
reading, playing a musical instrument, even immersing yourself
in your work, can help by taking your mind away from your
preoccupations and reminding you of things you do well.

What about the Children?

Many parents have told me that their children pulled them
through. Reach out past your pain to your children. Love them,
care for them—remember that they are hurting too. And play
with them. Their laughter, mischief, love of fun may help you to
smile and laugh again.

Almost all children have special needs during the separation
phase of divorce. Parents are sometimes relieved, even euphoric
to break out of a hostile, stifling, or loveless marriage. The
children, even when they have witnessed or been involved in
hostility or violence, are rarely happy. While most children get
over their acute reactions to the breakup within a year, the wish
or fantasy to return to the intact family often persists indefi-
nitely. Fears, both realistic and unrealistic, haunt many of them.
The family has been a protective womb for them. Loss of this
protection creates feelings of vulnerability, sadness, and helplessness. Many children feel guilty about things they did, or
imagine they did, that may have caused their parents' fights.
Most worry over their parents' obvious or hidden distress, and
may angrily denounce the parent they feel is to blame. Even
today, when divorce is common, many children feel "different," embarrassed, and shamed by their parents' behavior.

Every child's reaction is unique, a complex combination of
age, personality, and family dynamics. Chapter 7 will help you
to assess your children's strengths and vulnerabilities in order to
meet their individual needs.

Talk to Your Children

If, as research clearly shows, even two-year-old children show
less confusion and disruption if their parents tell them what is
happening, then thoughtful, open communication with older

children must be even more helpful. The fact is that expert after expert says, "Be honest with your children. Tell them, without guilt or blame and in terms they can understand, what is happening. Give them some warning of the big changes in their lives, then reassure them afterward. Don't just talk to them once. Go over and over these vital issues until you know they really understand, and then stay open to them, alert to their spoken and unspoken questions and concerns, ready to hear their worries and explain and assure again."

However, in my experience, few children are told enough. I have asked hundreds of children what their parents have told them about the separation or divorce. Although many of these children know far more than their parents suspect about their parents' lives, few remember their parents telling them anything. Perhaps one in five says, "Oh yeah, my dad came to my bedroom and said he was going away, and that he still loved me." Many have overheard parental arguments, fights, and complaints to others, and formed their own conclusions. Few have been told a fraction of what they have heard.

I asked the father of one very depressed boy why he had not talked to his son about leaving the family. The father replied, "I'm in constant psychic communication with my son!" Although this father may not be typical in his mode of communication, he is all too typical in the amount of information and understanding he is getting across to his children.

Parents justify their lack of communication by saying that their children do not want to talk about these things. Yet, just like adults, children are reminded frequently of their hurts by sounds, places, or events. A sensitive parent will be able to recognize when a child is thinking about the divorce, and take that opportunity to listen and talk. A concerned parent will not let a child's anxiety and discomfort derail a much-needed talk.

What should children be told? It does not need to be complicated, and of course it needs to be from your heart and in your own words. The basic ideas: Mother and Father are not able to live together any more. Why? Because we are very unhappy staying together. Mother or Father is going to move away, but he or she still loves you and will still be with you frequently. Together, Mother and Father will make sure that you will continue to be cared for. If a child asks, "Is it my fault?" or promises always to be good if only you will come back, it is important to emphasize that your decision had nothing to do with the child's behavior.

Remember, too, that children need to be listened to with great care. Children often voice their deepest concerns tentatively if at all, hiding them in innocent-sounding questions or behind symbols. If Teddy Bear cannot sleep, the bear's owner may be scared. If there are angry monsters in her room, there may be similar monsters in her feelings.

Older children may be more able to ask direct questions and can understand much more. A young child may ask, "Who will tuck me into bed?" and need reassurance that Mommy and Daddy will still take care of him. Older children may want to know if they will be living with Dad or Mom, and may have very practical reasons for wanting to know. My advice is to be honest about the facts of the situation—they will be clear to the children soon enough. At the same time, I advise every parent not to share angry, blaming, vengeful feelings with their children. These emotions are a natural and central part of separation, but they need to be expressed and worked through among adults and in the privacy of your own heart, not dumped on the children.

If children had their way, few parents would divorce. However, once children recognize the inevitability of their parents' separation, they almost always want to stay in close contact with both parents. Their instincts appear to be right, since psychological research has shown that, except in divorced families with the highest levels of ongoing conflict, children do best when they continue to spend time with both parents. Many states have written this important psychological finding into the law. Most custody laws now encourage "frequent and continuing contact" between the children and both parents.

Many parents, especially in the chaotic separation period, distance themselves from their ex-spouse *and* their children.

There are many reasons for this behavior, but none of them changes the fact that such distancing deprives the children of love, support, and reassurance at their time of greatest need. Stay in close touch with your children, even if it is difficult or painful. They need you.

Finding Common Ground

In the long run, the best way to minimize the trauma of separation and divorce for yourself and your children is to deal with your ex-spouse fairly and with respect. The sooner you let go of the attachments and animosities of your marriage and separation and start to build a new, businesslike relationship, the better.

Realistically, however, it is vital to recognize that treating your ex-spouse well does not guarantee equally good treatment in return. For reasons neither of you may be able to predict, understand, or control, the marital breakdown may be so unacceptable, threatening, or infuriating to your spouse that he or she acts in ways that are truly unacceptable to you, or that threaten the children. Before or after separation, your ex-spouse may form alliances with peers, family members, a counselor, or an overly aggressive attorney that cause hostile, erratic, or unfair actions. In some cases, long-standing emotional problems may flare to destructive levels. Under such circumstances, there are no simple solutions, only directions that are more or less constructive. To protect yourself and your children right now, you may need the leverage that only capable legal intervention can provide. At the same time, your longer-term interests require that the legal power you gain be used as judiciously as possible.

Businesslike Communication

During this period of time you and your ex-spouse have a lot of emotional and practical work to do. To sort out your relationship and your feelings, the two of you may need to do more soul-searching alone or together. You may need to talk together, on your own or in counseling, to understand the marriage and what went wrong, to finalize (or revoke) the decision to separate, to deal with all the disappointments, losses, and hurts—in other words, to carry on the work of emotional separation. At the same time, vital decisions must be made. Who stays in the house and who leaves? When? On a temporary basis, how much time will the children spend with each of you? On what kind of schedule? How can possessions, savings, and income be divided and stretched to create and support two homes?

The single most important decison that needs to be hammered out as soon as possible is to agree on *how to proceed*. Are the two of you going to negotiate, working out separation, support, and custody matters on your own? Or can you agree to find and work with a mediator, or choose two understanding, family-oriented attorneys to represent you? Can you agree on some form of principled dispute resolution? Or will you end up hiring aggressive advocates to do battle for you? If you and your ex-spouse can agree, even as you are separating, on *how* you will work things out later, you will be laying the groundwork for a successful separation.

Kenneth, a man I worked with, was so angry at his wife June for "deserting the family" that he could not talk to her without blowing up, even with the support of a counselor. At the same time, he desperately wanted to put his own and the children's lives back together again as quickly and constructively as possible. After agonizing about how to proceed, he wrote to his wife recognizing her determination to go back to school, restating his anger, and emphasizing his determination to keep the children from being hurt. He listed issues they urgently needed to work out, finances, legal steps, and child care. He suggested two ways to proceed, either through mediation or by finding two sensitive family lawyers to help them negotiate an agreement. He made it clear that his alternative would be to initiate legal proceedings. June responded by agreeing to mediation. In that setting they were able to come to adequate temporary agreements.

From the start, your emotional work and your business matters need to be separated—they are two different worlds. If they are allowed to collide, the results can be catastrophic. Set aside times and places for any needed exchanges about the relationship, about the two of you. Then fence these off from your talks about practical things. Who gets the color TV needs to be separate from what happened in New York five years ago. The issue of how much time the children spend with Mom and Dad should not be linked to what went on between Mom and Dad in their marriage.

How Honest Can You Be?

Abigail Trafford, author of *Crazy Time: Surviving Divorce*, points out that deception is intimately involved in nearly every marital crisis. As one or both partners grow and change, the relationship can stay alive only by changing too. If the growth goes underground, is hidden consciously or unconsciously, the marriage is headed for a breakup. As she points out, "When the marriage cracks, the past games of deception and denial are exposed."

Navigating the treacherous waters of separation requires taking a stand on a critical and extremely difficult issue—how honest can you be with the person from whom you are separating? For many, this question never comes up. In marriage after marriage, divorce after divorce, it is answered in the negative before ever being asked; the possibility of honesty is never really considered. If the idea of honesty does manage to flare up into awareness, it is quickly extinguished by the suffocating cloud of mistrust that surrounds almost every separating couple. "He would never understand." "She would use it against me." "He would interpret it as weakness." "She couldn't deal with the truth."

Why take the risks and face the pain of being honest about what you are feeling, thinking, and doing? For a very simple reason. When two parents separate, their mutual goal must be to bring their marital relationship to an end and to build a new, businesslike relationship concerning their children. The only kind of parent-parent relationship capable of protecting, nourishing, and guiding your children is one built on mutual trust. You children's needs require you to take the risks of openness.

The alternative is not to communicate, or to lie about what is really going on. If you choose not to talk to your ex-spouse, you make it impossible to correct the misperceptions about each other that spring up so easily. You see your ex-partner acting "crazy"—enraged, frightened, hysterical, out of control. Your ex-partner sees you the same way. As Johnston, Campbell, and Tall make clear, "It is not surprising, then, in the absence of corrective feedback (the spouses are usually no longer talking at this point) . . . that beliefs become rigidly fixed. Moreover, they form the presuppositions upon which any subsequent inter-action proceeds."

The first step, then, in dealing with the feelings of your ex-spouse, is to be as honest as possible. If you can avoid deception and "surprises," can reach the point where you have nothing to hide, you will minimize the mutual paranoia that grips many separating couples.

How Tolerant Can You Be?

The next step is to keep in mind that the off-the-wall things your ex-spouse is saying or doing do not tell the whole story. The extremes that people go through in the early stages of divorce should be so well known that nobody is surprised by them. However, when it is your ex-spouse who is euphoric one day and depressed the next, who rages at you today and seduces you tonight, who throws years of commitment and responsibility in the wastebasket and runs away, who flaunts a younger-and-thinner new mate, or a whole series of them, dives into a "this-is-it" religious group, or finds some other "crazy" thing to do, it is tempting to write them off. "That's the way they *really* are, and really were all the time," we tell ourselves. "They deserve whatever I can dish out."

On the other hand, if you can give yourself *and* your ex-spouse time to get through "the crazies" without carving your mistakes in stone, you will have taken a big step towards a winning solution for all of you.

Power, Provocation, and Peace

One of the most provocative things you can do is to act uni-
laterally in an area that requires joint decision making. Similarly, the provocations you will find hardest to deal with will be
when your ex-spouse does the same. The remedy—adequate
communication, advance warning, negotiation, agreement on
mutual issues—is simple, but it is frequently never tried
because of lack of trust, refusal to communicate, or power
games.

Power, who is in control, is a factor in every marriage. In
healthy relationships the partners find a livable balance of
power. When relationships break down, the power balance is up
for grabs, often the biggest issue. The partner who tired of
giving in may resolve never to be manipulated or coerced again,
and may act provocatively just to prove his or her independence.
"I won't do it and you can't make me" becomes the watchword.
This stuggle for power may be extremely threatening to the
once-dominant partner, who predictably fights even harder to
stay on top. At best, this power struggle leads to a hostile
standoff, a cold war in which nothing constructive gets done
because no one can agree without "backing down." At worst, it
can lead to life-threatening confrontations. I vividly remember a
picture that was on the front page of papers across North
America. It showed a man brandishing a knife, dangling his
two-year-old son out an apartment window. This is the ultimate
expression of an uncontrolled struggle for power.

The only way I know to escape from this trap is to use all your
feelings and power to focus on *what is right,* not *who is right.*
Your children need security and stability. How can it be a defeat
for either you or your ex-spouse to find a way to provide that?
Your children need to be supported at the highest level your
family can afford. Is it a sign of weakness to negotiate that
settlement? Your children need to be well fed, adequately
clothed, to live in an adequate home and neighborhood. How
can a parent "lose" in working, even with someone you hate, to
provide that?

Find Out What You and Your Ex *Really* Want

In the welter of feelings that surround separation, it is next to impossible to find which of your urgently competing needs and desires you really want to express. It will take months, even years, to sort out things of lasting value from the passing excitements of newfound freedom, for resilience and self-reliance to replace resentment and blame. For many, separation allows, or is in part caused by, a kind of adult adolescence, a new period of expansion, exploration, and change, and with those upheavals, moodiness, uncertainty about self, and acting out.

Looking back on this period, parent after parent has said to me, "I am so glad that I stayed close to my children. They pulled me through as much as I pulled them through. I am so proud of them." Sadly, some parents have shaken their heads and admitted, "I let my children slip away from me. I missed years of their lives. I realize now that I let my hurt and anger push them away. Now, when I see them, I'm a guest, not a parent."

Again, if you keep asking yourself, "What do I *really* want?" and listening to the answers from within, those answers are likely to be the guides you need. How many parents, in their hearts, do not want their children to be loved, safe, and secure? Achieving this, establishing your home as a safe, nurturing place for you and your children, establishing yourself as a truly independent adult, cannot be done by making war, however powerfully. It can only be done by using all of your power to make a new peace.

Explore Options—Search for a Win-Win Solution

A basic task during the period of separation is to explore a wide range of options concerning childcare, custody, living arrangments, and finances. At this time of rapid change, it is difficult or impossible to predict what your resources or needs will be very far in the future. It is also hard to predict how your children will respond to the stresses of separation or to any particular custody plan. So it makes good sense to be willing to experiment, provided that there is some agreed-upon way to determine whether a particular plan is working or not.

It is important to realize that meaningful shared parenting does not require a fifty-fifty division of the children's time. School and work schedules, the availability of child care, the distance between the two homes, and the needs of individual children and parents often make unequal divisions of time much better for all concerned. Appendix II describes a variety of age-appropriate parenting plans.

Shared parenting options, however, may not be the best solutions for everyone. Perhaps one parent really needs several years to devote full time to school or a new career. One parent may be going through an emotional crisis so severe that he or she has nothing to give to the chiildren for a period of time. Perhaps both parents strongly prefer providing their children the seemmingly simpler pattern of one "main" home, one "primary" parent to deal with. The child may be very young, still nursing, for example, and not able to cope with two homes or a more complicated schedule. Perhaps the children are in their teens and are clear that what they want is something else entirely. Two children may have very different needs; one may need to spend significantly more time with one parent than the other. Perhaps the availability of a grandparent or other caregiver, access to a particular school, or some other factor indicates that a more traditional arrangement would be better.

It has been my experience, supported by many research studies, that children will adjust to almost any custody arrangement *that is supported by both parents*. Do not close off options because you assume or are told "the kids can't cope." Find an option that promises to work for all concerned. If you and your ex-spouse can agree to give it an honest try, chances are the children will adjust to it better than you expect.

Exploring options is equally vital when it comes to money. Any financial advisor will tell you that your family's financial resources can be utilized far more effectively when there is agreement than when there is conflict. There are innumerable options when it comes to taxes, financing and refinancing, exchanges of property in and out of a marital settlement, the evaluation of businesses, professions, retirement funds, and inheritances. In a businesslike climate, these options can be explored, expert advice sought and utilized, and optimal solutions found. If conflict triumphs over common sense, chances are good that, by the time a judge decides for you, your lawyers will get more money than either you or your children.

Resolve Conflict through Negotiation or Mediation

As you separate, many issues need to be decided. These may include the separation itself—is it really going to happen, is it viewed as temporary or permanent, as an experiment or as leading to divorce? The separation is likely to *mean* something entirely different to you and to your spouse. You may see it as a chance to catch your breath, to make your partner appreciate you more. He or she may see it as an unforgivable betrayal or humiliation, an irrevocable step. Many practical matters, some with serious legal implications, need to be decided on a temporary basis and in a way that does not rule out different solutions in the future. All of these issues are best handled by thoughtful discussion, mediation, and negotiation.

In separating, you may feel enormous pressure to act, act quickly, and act on your own. Many separations do not even start as such; some people slam the door behind them in the heat of an argument and just never come back. However your separation happened, or at whatever stage you are now in, it is not too late to begin to pick up the scattered pieces and start to talk about them.

You have already been introduced to the idea of principled negotiation. The following dialogue shows how this method can be applied to separation issues. See if you can tell the win-win from the win-lose negotiator.

Mary: I think we need a separation.

Greg: If that's what you want, then go ahead. Just don't plan on seeing me or the children again.

Mary: I know that this is hurting you a lot, but I don't feel I have a real choice. I need some time by myself to think things through, but this has nothing to do with the children.

Greg: I'm not hurt, I just think you're sick. You're abandoning us, and you're going to pay for it.

Mary: You're threatening me, and that scares me. But one thing I can't do any more is to give in to your threats. That's been part of our problems for a long time. What I want us to do is find a solution.

Greg: How is running out on us a solution?

Mary: I'm not running away, I'm making a decision that I hope will give us both a break from our fighting. I won't be going far away. I'm willing to talk to you any time. And I certainly plan to stay close to the kids.

Greg: If you leave me then you're leaving the kids.

Mary: I've always thought we were both good parents. I think it's really important for us to solve our problems without hurting the kids. Isn't that what you want too?

Greg: Of course I don't want to hurt the kids. You're doing enough of that by leaving them.

Mary: Greg, I'm talking about separating from you, not abandoning our children. Are you willing to talk about us and the children separately?

Greg: How can we do that?

I think it is clear that the principled negotiator, by tenaciously sticking with the issues, by refusing to be provoked or manipulated by threats or guilt, was at least as powerful as her angry and reactive spouse. It may seem that nothing was accomplished in this exchange. However, the principled negotiator has demonstrated that threats and manipulation will not get results, and has modeled a far better way of solving problems. She has insisted on dealing with the problem rather than attacking the other person, sought for shared values, and avoided defending hardened positions. Although these parents have just begun to explore the option of separation and have not yet agreed on whether they should separate, or on what that separation will mean, by negotiating they have moved from reflexively using the children as a threat to recognizing a shared value—solving their problems without hurting the children.

Decisions that have legal implications may be particularly difficult to make during the storm of separation. The hardest is often a temporary agreement about care of and access to the children. Legal and emotional issues may make even a temporary solution to this problem hard to find.

Temporary Custody Agreements

As soon as possible, it it desirable to negotiate a temporary custody agreement that protects the children and both parents. All of the principles of negotiation already discussed will be of help in this. In addition, *referring to an objective standard* may be a crucial step in this area.

One standard on which temporary custody can be based is the history of parenting before the separation. A couple who have shared the day-to-day care and responsibility for the children relatively equally might structure a temporary agreement maintaining that status quo as workably as possible. A more traditional couple, in which one parent has been primarily responsible for the children since birth, might structure temporary plans reflecting that pattern.

For many families, however, the way things have been may not be an adequate model for the future. A parent who has been the primary caretaker for years may be leaving in part to pursue school, career, or personal involvements independently of the children. Conversely, when education, career, or dysfunctional marital patterns have isolated a parent from the children, he or she may sincerely hope to deepen the parent-child relationship, and the children may benefit if that happens. For these couples, a temporary custody agreement could reflect a shared value, a future goal, perhaps of equally shared custody, or an acceptable and workable compromise between the historical pattern and plans for the future.

With couples who can cooperate concerning their children, I encourage them to be willing to try out one or more proposed custody plans, monitoring their own and the children's adjustment to them. However, along with most counselors, I strongly advise against frequent redefinitions of custody, particularly when these redefinitions are forced through litigation. Children need stability, and one absolutely vital foundation for such stability is lasting parental agreement concerning their schedules, placement, and care.

Your temporary custody agreement can include statements about your values, goals, and plans concerning the children, along with a description of the custody and timesharing plan itself. Although variations from state to state make it desirable to get legal advice and assistance in drawing up this agreement, most courts will now respect a reasonable custody plan worked out by the parents. Once such a plan is court ordered, it does set a precedent for the future. However, clear statements concerning agreed-upon goals (for example, equal time with the children as soon as both parties have adequate homes) should provide enough protection to allow a couple to separate without jeopardizing either parents' relationship with the children. In Chapter 9 you will find a sample of this kind of parenting agreement.

If you and your ex-spouse can emerge from the period of separation as two healthy individuals, with communication lines still open, with a working level of mutual trust, and with the outlines of a constructive parenting plan, you will have built a solid foundation for your own and your children's future.

A Parent's Voice

Sitting under a tree outside her home, while her six-year-old roughhoused with his dog, one mother summed up her experience of the separation process.

> At first it was awful! I spent a lot of days in this house crying, not even going out. It was very scary starting over. I don't think I would have made it if I didn't have a fifteen-month-old kid to keep myself going for.
>
> I got to be pretty good at locking things away that I had no control over. I couldn't see what was happening at my ex's house. I finally realized that my choices were to make myself absolutely crazy and miserable or do the best job that I could while Josh was with me, and hope that his Dad was going to do the same thing. I think it goes back to self-

preservation. I realize that I only had so much energy. Why squander it on something I couldn't control no matter how hard I tried?

I had to learn, relearn, how to make my own decisions. Now I realize that our separation was an incredible opportunity for growth, for looking at everything I did and deciding if I really wanted to keep doing it or not.

In the midst of that kind of change, I found that I needed to develop a process, because my foundations were being threatened. It was frightening, but acceptable, because I was the one who was threatening them. I saw that if I was risking all of my old stability, I'd better develop a decision-making process that I could count on, that I knew was unshakable.

I would deliberately wait a week to think things through. I would let it run through my mind. I would talk to the people I trusted. I would write it down. Now it seems artificial, but then it gave me the inner stability and certainty I needed.

You know, I just wrote a letter to my cousin who's going through her own divorce. I just meant to write a few words, but I ended up writing her a long letter. What did I end up telling her? I told her to eat well, sleep a lot, and find out who her real friends are. And that it gets easier. It gets better.

CHAPTER 7

Your Children's Needs: What You Don't Know Can Hurt Them

What does divorce look like and feel like to a child? Divorce hurts children, some of them profoundly. Without warning or explanation, a child's home and family are shattered, the two most important people in the world separated, often with great anger and sorrow. Caught in their own problems, the parents have less to give; sometimes one of them is lost to the child completely. The intact family that has been the foundation of the child's world is gone forever.

The Invisible Child

One theme that unhappy children from both intact and divorced families share is "invisibility"—someone they love and depend upon is unable to see, appreciate, and respond to them for what they are. Their real needs get lost, their signals are misread or missed entirely, their pleas go unnoticed. Many things can blind parents to their children's real needs: abuse when they themselves were children, serious physical or emotional illness, grinding poverty, severe personal trauma, and, high on the list, divorce.

Judy Reed, a gifted counselor who works with many children of divorce, traces many of the problems she sees—withdrawal and depression, physical illness, self-destructive behavior, anxiety, fears, inability to get along with peers or with authority figures—to the powerlessness and confusion that this invisibility causes:

Some of them are really in despair. There's this real sense
of hopelessness about having any sort of impact in their
own lives. Everyone else makes the decisions for them and
they just have to go along. Their parents, particularly the
ones who are involved in custody battles, are so involved in
themselves and "the other"—the ex-spouse—that they
either overfocus on the child, or don't have the time to
spend with them. The child as a whole person gets lost,
and whatever it is the parent wants—to get even, to be
right, to win custody—controls everything. So the issues
that need to be dealt with for the sake of the child get
overshadowed by the parents' own issues. The kids get
caught right in the middle, so they're the ones that come
out like swiss cheese. When the bullets are flying, the kids
get hit.

The antidote to invisibility, powerlessness, anger, and despair
is for parents to continue to see, understand, and respond to
their children through all the stages of divorce. As a parent you
are one of the few people whose loving vision has the power to
nurture and protect your child. To a degree, the way you see
your child actually forms and molds him or her. If you see and
nurture the goodness and strength in your child it will flower; if
all you can see are your child's imperfections and flaws, those
too will grow. If, caught in your own overwhelming troubles,
your children's needs become invisible to you, their development cannot help but be disrupted. Your child needs your
understanding like a plant needs the sun.

As a frequent visitor to preschool classrooms, I have been
struck by how different children are. A class full of four-year-
olds has an amazingly wide range of youngsters. Some are
active and sociable, their smiles and energy drawing other
children to them. Others, equally energetic, frustrate and anger
their classmates by pushing, grabbing, screaming, or crying.
Some children play happily by themselves for long periods,
others constantly interact with their peers or seek attention from
adults. Some are bold, quick to try any new activity, eager to

explore. Others hang back cautiously, needing to watch for a long time before being coaxed to try something new. In any room there are leaders and followers, happy children and despondent ones, quick learners and slow learners, shy children and social stars.

Part of being a good parent is having an acute sense of each of your children as individuals. This awareness means looking past cultural stereotypes—not every boy is or should be a football player, nor every girl a nurse; past family stereotypes—Smiths don't cry, Joneses are artistic; and beyond your own ego—"my child is just like me." It means spending time with your children, not directing or teaching, but listening and watching. It means being open to the informed views of those who know your child in different ways, teachers, counselors, or other professionals. In a divorce it may mean making a special effort to see your child through your ex-spouse's eyes as well as through your own.

Personality Patterns

New York pediatricians Alexander Thomas and Stella Chess noticed that some children cause parents very little trouble, while others are the source of endless difficulties. Years of research have allowed them to identify certain patterns of temperament that describe many children. These distinctive, relatively stable characteristics are very useful in attempting to predict how children will cope with their parents' divorce, and in structuring parenting plans that meet children's individual needs.

"Easy" Kids

Many children adjust easily and well to most of the changes and demands in their lives. These children typically approach new situations and people readily, adapt to new situations without difficulty, are usually cheerful, show responses that are not overly intense, and are relatively regular and predictable in their habits. About four children out of ten are blessed with this benign cluster of qualities. It is not surprising that these easygoing children have relatively few problems unless the demands that are made on them in different parts of their life are simply too contradictory.

If your child is this kind of easy child, then your divorce, while stressful, does not have to be destructive to him or her. As long as changes are not too abrupt and unexpected, or the expectations of the parents too contradictory, your child has what it takes to cope with and adjust to your divorce and new family structure. A variety of parenting plans can be considered and evaluated with the expectation that your child will handle any reasonable arrangement relatively well.

"Difficult" Kids

Parents with easy children often do not realize how lucky they are until they have a difficult child, a child who is endowed with a package of temperamental traits that are the opposite of those of their "easy" brothers and sisters.

Difficult children—about one child in ten—tend to shy away from new situations and new people. It takes them a long time and requires much parental encouragement before they settle into a new pattern. They are often sad, angry, or in some other unhappy mood. To make matters worse, they tend to express their feelings intensely, and their eating, sleeping, and other habits are changeable and unpredictable. As any parent of a child like this will agree, these youngsters are hard to deal with adequately under the best of conditions; under the bombardment of divorce, they are at high risk for developing serious emotional and behavioral problems, and for adding their own problems to those of their already-overburdened parents.

These difficult children are simply not equipped to cope with intense or protracted hostilities between their parents. Nor are they as able as many children to adjust to unstable or less-than-ideal living arrangements. If severe problems are to be avoided, parents need to put their own needs aside to help these vulnerable children through the divorce transition with patience and care.

"Slow-to-Warm-Up" Kids

Perhaps 15 percent of children fall in this third group. While their initial reactions to new people and new situations tend to be negative, these responses are not overly intense. In addition, these children are more predictable in their sleep patterns, eating, and other habitual activities than their difficult siblings. Alert parents of these children will have learned to be patient and persistent in encouraging them to get used to new foods, new friends, school, and new activities. The payoff for this persistent parenting approach is to see one's slow-to-warm-up child blossom and thrive once a challenge is mastered.

The sudden, unexpected changes that divorce can cause are very disruptive to these children. They need advance warning of large and small changes in their lives. Predictably their first reactions to a new custody or time-sharing plan will be negative. However, if their protests are listened to with understanding and they are encouraged by both parents to "give it a try," they may surprise everyone by eventually making an excellent adjustment.

The Developmental Dance

No two children progress at exactly the same rate, and every child is farther ahead in some areas than in others. For example, one child might be advanced in speech, but behind in fine coordination, while a second might be a social whiz, but slow in developing academic skills.

It often helps parents to think of each child's pace of development along several different "tracks." Some important developmental areas are:

Physical: height, weight, vigor, and strength.
Large motor coordination: sitting up, crawling, walking, running, riding, throwing, etc.
Fine motor coordination: eye-hand coordination, self-feeding, scribbling, coloring, drawing, writing, manipulation.

Receptive language: attending to, responding to, and understanding voices, words, and speech.

Expressive language: making expressive sounds, using words, naming objects, colors, etc., speaking meaningfully and expressively.

Daily living: self-care, dressing, toilet training, cleanliness, grooming, following safety and household rules, etc.

Social: interest in and response to others, learning to interact and play with other children, interacting with adults.

Academic: motivation and ability to pay attention, sit still, follow directions, join in learning activities, work independently, and benefit from school.

Aptitude for learning: rate of mastery of reading, spelling, writing, mathematics, and other academic skills.

General adaptation: the overall quality of your child's adjustment and coping in a variety of situations and at various times—"common sense," "getting along," "street smarts."

If your child has progressed at roughly the same rate as other children in these ten areas, it suggests a relatively healthy and resilient young person. Normal or early development indicates that your child has vital resources to draw upon when needed. However, a serious delay, consistently late or inadequate achievement of skills in one or more areas over much of your child's life, indicates that your child requires some specialized, ongoing help. The delays or problems of which you are aware should be discussed with your child's pediatrician, teachers, or other professionals.

For example, a child who has been consistently late at each stage of language use, and who currently is significantly less fluent and expressive than other children the same age, could almost certainly benefit from evaluation and systematic help by a speech and language therapist. This child may also need specialized testing and help at school. If a developmental lag is severe enough, a child may need focused attention from parents and professionals over a period of years.

Similarly, moderate or serious delays in several areas of development create an additional challenge for a child and his or her parents. Many children with developmental delays go on to lead happy and successful lives. However, their successes are almost always built on realistic recognition of their problems, close coordination with physicians, other professionals, and the schools, and years of hard work by capable and caring parents.

The stresses of divorce often hit a child where he or she is most vulnerable. A young child with slow language development may regress to baby talk, a child with learning problems may fail at school. If you feel that your child has significant developmental delays, special needs above and beyond those of others the same age, his or her future may well depend on what you and your ex-spouse do about them right now.

Infants

A child's responses to separation and divorce are strongly shaped by age and developmental level. Babies are sensitive to any impairments in the consistency and adequacy of their basic care. They respond to reduced or erratic parenting with fretfulness and crying, eating and digestive problems, development delays or regression, and in extreme cases, failure to thrive.

Preschool Children

These children may be those who are most vulnerable to divorce-related stresses, often showing the most significant problems during the first year or two after separation. Young preschool children—in the 2½- to 3½-year-old range—often regress. They may move backwards in toilet training, show more irritability, whining, and crying, become afraid to be separated from a parent, and display increased masturbation, aggression, or tantrums. It is important to remember that even for children this young, being talked to, receiving explanations that help them understand what is happening, can help to minimize their problems.

Five- to six-year-olds on the whole are more able to understand what is happening to them. Nonetheless, they often become anxious, fearful, moodier, and more aggressive. Many are intensely sad about the loss of their family, particularly if separation means little or no contact with one parent. Often children this age cover up their depressed and fearful feelings with unconvincingly bubbly and happy facades. They say they are "always happy," that "everybody" loves them, but these same children may lose their ability to play, worry incessantly about being replaced, develop phobias, or seek reassurance by clinging to strangers or climbing into their laps. When they can express it, many convey an overwhelming sense of helplessness and loss.

School-age Children

School children, ideally, have freed up much of their energy from the intense family involvements of the earliest years, and are ready and able to absorb the rich, new experiences offered by educational activities, schoolmates, and teachers. Unfortunately, many children of divorce are cut off from this by anger, sadness, and fear. Wallerstein and Kelly found that some children in this age range become immobilized. Unable to master their powerful feelings of deprivation, they use fantasies of reconciliation to avoid dealing with a reality that is too threatening. Although some of these children become very angry at the parent they blame for their losses, more often school-age children feel intense loyalty to both parents. These are the children who are most damaged by ongoing parental arguments or by one parent's continuing criticism of the other.

Older school-age children have an increasingly realistic understanding of their parents, the divorce, and what it means to them. They are also more able to take independent action to protect themselves from some of the impacts of divorce or, at times, to become central actors in the drama that is taking place. Many older children are intensely, often articulately angry. Wallerstein and Kelly report, "Approximately half of the children in this group were angry at their mothers, the other half at their fathers, and a goodly number were angry at both. Many of the children were angry at the parent whom they thought initiated the divorce, and their perception of this was usually accurate."

Preadolescent Children

It is in the preadolescent years, when children's anger can become wedded with a black-and-white sense of moral outrage and personal indignation, that one of the most tragic outcomes for children and parents occurs. Many of these youngsters—up to 80 percent in the highest-conflict families—come to reject one parent totally and absolutely.

"My father used to be okay, but he's turned into a monster," Scott, a serious, intelligent eleven-year-old explained to me. "He beat up my Mom three times, and I was there every time. He practically scared my little sister to death when he kicked down our door. He's made my Mom pay fifteen thousand dollars for our lawyer, just to keep us safe. When I used to go to his house, he would threaten me and Tammy if we didn't tell him everything Mom was doing. I don't ever want to see him again, not even when I'm grown up."

Scott, and many boys and girls like him, match their actions to their words. They beg and plead not to be made to visit the hated parent, get sick, throw tantrums, or run away to avoid contact, and, if forced, retreat into sullen unresponsiveness or berate the rejected parent for hours. In the strength and absolute quality of their stance, they become powerful, sometimes decisive figures in the ongoing battle between their parents. A stance like this, once solidified, may last for years.

Adolescents

As teenagers develop, they become more capable of understanding cause and effect, of grasping the psychological underpinnings of events. Many are keenly aware of and far more knowledgeable about the details and motives of their parents' lives than their parents like to think. Like their younger brothers and sisters, many feel a great sense of loss, although for them the loss includes what might have been in addition to what once was there.

We are all aware of teenagers' easily provoked sense of

embarrassment and shame. This reaction is painfully evident when the fact of, or even worse the facts about, their parents' divorce becomes public. In addition, teenagers often are deeply embarrassed *for* their parents, mortified by the childlike behaviour they see in them. Many develop increased resentment of younger siblings. Others, caught between a desire for contact with both parents and an age-appropriate need to spend time with their friends, are frustrated by almost any time-sharing agreements. Many resent not being consulted when these arrangements are made.

Many teens retreat to an exaggerated attitude of "playing it cool" to distance themselves from the conflicts of separation, while others, perhaps more constructively, bury themselves in friendships and activities. When these defenses break down and teenagers are unable to maintain an emotional distance from their parents' conflicts, they may become acutely withdrawn and depressed, or, with frightening results, out of control, assaultive, and violent.

What to Do?

It is important to realize that most children show most of these problems at some time or another. How many children have never been afraid of the dark or have never had a nightmare? How many parents have never worried about a child's eating patterns? Almost every child has been too aggressive at times, too shy at others. It is totally unrealistic to expect children to be happy all the time, never fearful, never overly active. If your ratings show a scattering of behavior problems, difficulties that have appeared now and then, in some situations but not in others, your child is probably adjusting about as well as other children. You can expect that, like most children, your child will be troubled by many aspects of your divorce, but you do not have to dread extraordinary difficulties.

However, if your child is showing clear problems in several areas, particularly if those problems began soon after your separation or become worse when divorce-related issues or conflicts come up, your child may be at increased risk from the stresses of your divorce. The problem behaviors you are seeing may stem from long-standing personality characteristics that make your child particularly vulnerable. Or they may indicate that your child, however strong and resilient by nature, is experiencing more confusion, loss, or conflict than he or she can handle.

Parents seldom like to learn that their child has a problem. Because it hurts to see one's child hurting, it is not unusual for parents to delay recognition of areas that need attention. Under the pressures of divorce, this temporary denial may be greatly exaggerated. Divorcing parents are prone to seeing their children as they need to see them, rather than as they are, denying obvious problems for self-serving reasons. Admitting a child's problem, for example, might be felt as an unacceptable failure, be used as ammunition in court, create unwanted responsibilities, or represent giving in to the other parent. Sometimes divorcing parents do just the opposite, exaggerating a child's problems, usually to "prove" that the other parent is abusive, neglectful, or inadequate, or that an inconvenient or disliked pattern of custody or contact is not working.

If temperamental, developmental, or behavioral problems are ignored, particularly in the stress-filled period of divorce, they will almost certainly get worse. If minor problems are exaggerated, they may well develop into major ones. In either case, the real child remains invisible and vital needs go unmet. It is important for you and your ex-spouse to talk to and listen to your child, and to help her or him with all the parental skills you have. Frequently, however, the children of divorce need professional help in the form of play therapy, individual counseling, or family therapy.

If you and your ex-spouse can continue to see your children clearly and lovingly throughout the months or years of divorce, they need not become invisible, confused, or helpless. If you can continue to see both their problems and their potentials, you can accomplish a vital task that nobody else can do as well—to know and love your children for what they are, while helping them to grow into what they can be.

When Children Do Best

Children do best when:
- their parents solve custody, contact, and financial problems quickly and efficiently.
- they are protected from parental conflicts.
- their parents transform conflict into cooperation.
- they feel free to love and respect both parents.
- they can maintain close, consistent contact with both parents.
- both parents remain physically and emotionally healthy.
- neither parent suffers a major drop in standard of living.
- they are talked to and listened to throughout the process of divorce.
- they do not have to fill adult roles as confidants, caretakers, or co-conspirators.
- their individual and developmental needs continue to be met.

CHAPTER 8

Win-Win-Win-Negotiating

It took us more than a year to work out our custody plan, and some
of our talks were really hard. I would shake inside, I was so upset.
But when we finished it all up, Dave came over to me, gave me a
hug, and told me that he still loved me. We both knew for a long
time that we couldn't go back, but that let me see him as a human
being again, someone I didn't have to be afraid of. Then I knew the
kids and I—we'd be okay.
—Carol, age thirty-four

There are three central parties to a divorce—a mother, a father,
and their children. A "win-win-win" solution means that all
three come through this storm alive and well. In the intimate,
tightly bonded world of a family, this outcome can happen only
when a fair and realistic solution is reached through an equally
fair, efficient, and nondestructive process. A family just cannot
afford a custody war.

Getting Started

Negotiation requires communication—sitting down and talking. If you and your ex-spouse are both committed to negotiating a mutually acceptable parenting plan, then little more is
needed to begin than to agree on a time and a place. But what if
you want to negotiate and your ex-spouse does not? Or even
worse, what if you want to negotiate and your ex-spouse wants
to nail you to the wall? It will not help to complain about how
unfair and irrational he or she is, or to give yourself moral credit
for being right and reasonable. No one, not even the judge, is

104

going to notice how good you are being and solve the problem for you—*nobody is keeping score*. If you want to work things out and your ex-spouse does not, you almost certainly will need to apply power to make this happen.

Are You Powerful or Powerless?

An observer might note that there are two kinds of people in the world, those who are comfortable wielding power and those who are not. A cynic might add that these two kinds of people usually end up married to each other. A surprising number of adults have never learned to stand up for themselves, to take steps in the face of someone else's disapproval, or to act independently. Even someone who is reasonably powerful in some areas may feel powerless because of the circumstances of a divorce. A parent may have moved out for very good reasons, but is now being depicted as an abandoning parent. One parent may control all or most of the financial resources, tilting the balance of power. One parent may threaten to move away with the children, leaving the other parent out in the cold.

Kate had this kind of problem. She lived in New York. Her ex-husband Howard and their three children had moved to Colorado. Although Howard had custody of the children, they had agreed that when the children reached their teens they could live with her if they wanted to. During their summer visit with her, the two older boys, 13 and 15, convinced her that they now wanted to move in with her. However, when Kate approached Howard about sending the boys to her, he not only refused, but refused even to talk about it. He hung up when she called, her letters went unanswered. As she put it, "I was pounding my head against a wall."

Although Kate did not want to create trouble for her ex-husband or the children, she could not give up and walk away. The boys wanted to live with her. She very much wanted more time with them. She knew she had a lot to offer them at this point in their lives.

Kate realized that she needed power just to get her ex-husband to talk to her about this. Appeals to his sense of fairness, to their prior agreement, and to the children's desires had not helped. She was tempted to try to stir up the children's feelings with guilt; she thought of bribing them with promises, and by now she was angry enough that it would have been easy to try to undermine their love and respect for their father by criticizing him to them or dramatizing how much he was hurting her. However, she knew that using the children in any of these ways would only hurt them. Her alternative, the only source of power she could find, was the legal system.

With care she selected an attorney who understood the whole range of uses of the law. He was experienced in the complexities of interstate custody law, he could "play hardball" when needed, and he was always open to constructive ways of resolving disputes. They moved forward very cautiously, giving her ex-husband advance warning of each step, asking for no more than they thought was fair, making no attempt to discredit or harm him. Most important, at each step they made it clear that negotiations could start at any time.

As legal procedures usually do, these took a long time. Almost a year went by without a solution. There were many times when Kate became infuriated by the delays or was tempted to give up. However, her attorney was wise and caring enough to counsel patience and persistence rather than encouraging her to act on impulse. Howard continued to "stonewall" on this issue until a few weeks before the scheduled custody hearing.

Just before the trial, his attorney offered to negotiate. Once Kate and her ex-husband started to talk, they were quickly able to agree on two constructive steps. They sought objective information about the children's needs and preferences from a neutral family therapist, and they agreed on a mediator. When mediation began, it became clear that there were potential benefits to everyone by making a change. The two older children would get some desirable time with their mother in a stimulating new environment, the youngest child would get some undiluted time with Dad, and Howard would be able to make some career steps that he had been putting off for a long time.

They never went to court, but they could not have reached a mutual solution without using the power that the court represents. Whenever there is more conflict than willingness to negotiate, some form of power must be used to motivate negotiation.

Assessing Your Power

You can evaluate your power relative to your ex-spouse by answering the following questions. If you and your ex-spouse are clearly different on an item, circle the appropriate person. If the two of you are about equal, or if the statement does not describe either of you accurately, circle "Same."

1. Who tends to see only one side of any issue? Self Ex Same
2. Who wants "peace at any price"? Self Ex Same
3. Who is more willing to disagree openly? Self Ex Same
4. Who tries harder to pacify the other? Self Ex Same
5. Who is more rigid and inflexible? Self Ex Same
6. Who is more likely to give in? Self Ex Same
7. Who is more blaming of the other? Self Ex Same
8. Who feels more inadequate and responsible? Self Ex Same
9. Who uses threats? Self Ex Same
10. Who fails to assert his or her own needs? Self Ex Same
11. When a choice is made, who usually "wins"? Self Ex Same
12. Who ends up feeling like a victim? Self Ex Same
13. Who is willing to confront? Self Ex Same
14. Who avoids conflict? Self Ex Same
15. Who controls the finances? Self Ex Same

16. Who is in worse straits finan-
    cially?   Self Ex Same
17. Who has more financial informa-
    tion and understanding?   Self Ex Same
18. Who feels more confused or over-
    whelmed?   Self Ex Same
19. Who defines or creates situations
    and issues?   Self Ex Same
20. Who is more eager to reach a set-
    tlement?   Self Ex Same

Scoring

A. Count the number of odd-numbered items circled "Self."

   My overt power =   _____

B. Count the number of odd-numbered items circled "Ex."

   Ex-spouse's overt power =   _____

C. Count the number of even-numbered items circled "Self."

   My tendency to accommodate = _____

D. Count the number of even-numbered items circled "Ex."

   Ex's tendency to accommodate = _____

The balance of power: compare your effective power (A + D) to your ex-spouse's effective power (B + C).

-----------	vs.	-----------
(A + D)		(B + C)
My Effective Power		Ex's Effective Power

If your power rating is within a point or two of that of your ex-spouse, your ratings do not reveal a marked power imbalance. Communications and negotiations may be hard, but the process should be fair. If your power rating is three or more points less than that of your ex-spouse, you see yourself on the short end of the power stick. Your ex-spouse seems to you to be the one who creates situations, defines issues, and dominates the decision-making process. You see yourself as more insecure or needy in terms of personal or financial resources. You may avoid conflict, feel poorly informed or overwhelmed, fail to assert your own needs, and attempt to pacify or placate your ex-spouse.

Before undertaking negotiations on your own behalf, you need to increase your power. A knowledgeable and effective attorney can add to your power through example and advice. Reviewing the twelve sources of power presented below will be useful. If you continue to feel powerless, you may need to rely on a forceful advocate to advance your own and your children's needs.

If you are significantly more powerful than your ex-spouse, you face a different risk. Negotiations may proceed to your liking and you may be able to push through an agreement that meets your needs very well, although almost certainly at the expense of your ex-spouse, and perhaps of the children as well. The danger here is that fear, anger, or resentment will push your ex-spouse to undermine or sabotage your agreement. He or she may be provoked to take desperate action, such as alienating or stealing the children. You may "win" the house, the car, the pension plan, custody, come out ahead on every issue, only to lose your children's love, or the children themselves.

Use your power to ensure that the process is fair. Push for principled mediation rather than one-sided solutions. Insist that your ex-spouse voice his or her real needs and feelings rather than bowing to yours. Make sure that your children's needs are understood and met before your own. Refuse to settle for anything short of a solution that is realistic, workable, and fair to all concerned.

Building Power

Power comes in many forms. Kate could have exerted power by bribing, encouraging, or tricking the children into making life miserable for Howard. She could have threatened to steal the children or to harm Howard's reputation. She could have exerted power by harassing and denigrating Howard, finding a way to hurt him financially, or by going to Colorado and actually stealing the children. She chose not to use any of these sources of power because, however frustrated and angry she felt, she never forgot that to do so would hurt the people she loved.

In a divorce, the obvious sources of power are money and the children. In the day-to-day reality of millions of divorce negotiations, these two factors are played against each other with little regard for other values. The partner with more money, most often the father, "buys" time with the children. The partner who needs money, usually the mother, "sells" access to the children in order to keep the house or gain more support. Sometimes this works out adequately, but too often this limited exchange becomes destructive. By threatening to sue for custody, one parent may induce the other to accept a settlement that locks that parent and the children into poverty. One parent can make communication and contact with the children so miserable that they are deprived of the other parent's love and support. However, you have access to many other sources of power whose careful use is far less destructive than simply pitting love against money. Some of these sources of power follow.

The Power of the Law

The court system, for all its flaws, is based on the idea of justice, on the belief that the powerful and the powerless are equal in the eyes of the law. I am convinced that most lawyers and judges, most of the time, make every effort to live up to this ideal. In practical terms, this equality before the law means that no one needs to give away basic rights. As long as you and your attorney are willing and able to go to court if you have to, then you should be able to get a fair share of the assets of your marriage and adequate contact with your children.

Professional negotiators use the acronym "BATNA," which stands for your "Best Alternative To a Negotiated Agreement." There is no reason to negotiate any settlement that is worse than your BATNA, worse than you could get some other way. In a divorce, your BATNA may well be what you can expect from a court. A lawyer experienced in how your local court handles family law cases can usually give you a reasonably clear idea of what to expect if your case has to go to court. That same attorney can make sure that if you do go to court, your interests are advocated clearly, understandably, and effectively.

It can be very destructive to use the threat of court manipulatively to frighten or coerce your ex-spouse into an unfair settlement. However, if your ex-spouse is avoiding any movement towards a solution, attempting to threaten, dominate, or control you, or acting destructively towards you or the children, it may be necessary to make it clear that you are willing to use the court system effectively, not to "win" for yourself, but to bring about a timely, workable, and fair solution.

An increasing number of states allow an attorney to be appointed to represent the children in a custody dispute. This can be an effective way of utilizing the power of the court to reach a custody decision that truly protects the children.

The Power of Being Right

Being right—consistently acting in a legitimate, evenhanded way—may give you power even without relying on the court. Most of us recognize fairness and restraint when we encounter it. An adversary who neither retaliates nor gives in when provoked sooner or later gains our respect. A parent who consistently refuses to hurt the children by bringing them into the battle, who diligently focuses on the children's needs, who never asks for more than is fair, will almost certainly make us more willing to cooperate. There is no guarantee that this will happen, but it is often surprising how powerful it can be to demonstrate, appeal to, and rely on mutual trust, respect for prior agreements, fairness, and shared love for your children.

The Power of Knowledge

Far too many parents go through the divorce in ignorance of absolutely vital information. They rely on their lawyers, but never find out what the law really says about child custody or finances. They may consult financial advisers, but never really understand what their resources or expenses are, what the law provides, what the tax consequences of various options would be, or what their decisions will mean five, ten, or twenty years later. They may take their children to see a therapist, but never find out what experts have to say about the variety of parenting plans that might work for their children. An amazing number of parents never talk to their children carefully enough to learn their real needs and feelings.

It pays to make yourself an expert on the issues that impact on you through your divorce. In negotiating, it is vital to generate and evaluate many alternatives. Without adequate information, the best solutions may never be proposed, and it is impossible to know what a proposed solution really means to you unless you have the knowledge to evaluate it. Building up your own knowledge and expertise has an important extra benefit—it is a potent antidote against feelings of powerlessness and depression.

Although you can learn a lot from reading, the most effective way to gain detailed, accurate, and usable information about the law, finances, taxes, and your children's special needs is by working with experts. Expert help can be expensive. However, I know of few more important investments that you can make if you want to be in control of what happens to you and your children.

Another helpful kind of knowledge, something you cannot get from experts, comes from other people who have been through similar experiences. If you feel that a shared parenting arrangement would be better for all of you, finding a local family that is doing well with a similiar plan can be more convincing than all the arguments in the world. Better yet, find several families, so you can compare what they are doing. Talk to other divorced or divorcing parents; find or put together a support group. Encourage your ex-spouse to do the same. You can learn a tremendous amount from the successes and failures of others.

Surprisingly, one of the easiest negotiations I ever mediated involved a lawyer and her ex-husband who had been fighting about money and custody for more than three years. By the time they came to me, they had become such experts on their situation that, once we got past their mutual anger, they were able to generate and evaluate options with ease. In the end, I had to do little more than write down their agreements as they made them.

The Power of Knowing the Other Person's Real Needs

Your ex-spouse may be insisting on fifty-fifty shared custody, which you feel is unworkable for your children. It is possible that the demand for equal time symbolizes a different, perhaps a deeper need. Your ex-spouse may feel that his or her worth as a parent was ignored throughout the marriage, and may really want meaningful recognition as a parent. If you can recognize that deeper need, you may be able to meet it in other ways—for example, by agreeing on joint legal custody, agreeing that all important decisions about the children will be shared, or by writing into your parenting agreement an explicit recognition of your mutual worth as parents.

The situation might easily be reversed. Your ex-spouse may know that your identity is based on being "the parent" to your children. For you, any solution that leaves you with other than sole custody of the children would be devastating. If your ex-spouse is well motivated towards you, he or she may go along with this deep need on your part. However, with less positive motivations, it becomes easy to demand concessions in terms of support or the division of property in exchange for the symbol of "sole custody."

It is also important to be fully aware of your own needs. If desperate finances or out-of-control feelings are pushing you towards a quick settlement, your urgency can work against you. Delay or the threat of delay could easily lead you to accept a settlement that is unfair to you or inadequate for the children. Similarly, if you have a need to avoid conflict at any cost, you can easily be coerced by threats, by confrontation, or by litigation. To the extent that you know what your real needs are, you may be able to meet them or deal with them in other ways. By doing that you will reown your lost power.

The Power of Understanding

During the years of your marriage, you were one of the most significant people in your ex-spouse's life. Whether times were good or bad, you would not have been together unless you meant a great deal to each other. Although your separation may have created great conflicts between you, your willingness even now to see things through his or her eyes, your ability to understand his or her point of view, may significantly help the two of you to reach a solution. Although an insincere "I understand" may accomplish nothing, the efforts you make to grasp the other person's reality add to the foundation of an eventual agreement.

One man I worked with told me how frustrated he had been because of his ex-wife's seemingly irrational refusal even to talk about selling their house. From his point of view, the house was an investment that was tying up most of their assets. When he became able to listen to his ex-wife, he realized that it represented her only stability in an extremely threatening time. He told her that he would stop pressuring her to sell the house if she would recognize his need for enough liquid assets to allow him to risk a much-needed job change. Working together, they were able to refinance the house, meeting both her needs for security and his needs for change.

The Power of Persistence

It does not make sense to continue to act in ways that are ineffective or harmful. However, it makes very good sense to make it clear that you will never give up working for what is fair and right for your children and yourself. By clinging fiercely to what you honestly believe is right, you serve notice that you cannot be pushed aside or swept away. Very often it is the person with the most patience and endurance whose views win out.

To persist in the face of the storms that divorce stirs up, it is vital that your basic needs are met. From the moment you decide to separate, you need not only tie down the basics as best you can—adequate financial support, emotional support, contact with your children, a place to live—but also to be sure of your hopes and plans. In the end, your own commitment to your goals is the real source of your power.

The Power of Support

While commitment and persistence are the powerhouses for realizing your hopes, the support you can gain from others serves to legitimize and add weight to your plans. This support can come at the personal level from friends and family, but also from people who know you as a person and as a parent.

Such accumulated support is particularly beneficial when a case does go to court. The court or court-appointed evaluators or conciliators may well turn to teachers, doctors, therapists, or others who know your family for crucial information. The teacher who has seen you bring and pick up your child on time for the past year has a lot to say about your reliability. The school psychologist who has seen you advocate attention to your child's needs and follow up on recommendations can attest to your active concern.

Many parents try to win support in a different way. They put their friends and family through the same test of loyalty that can be so destructive to their children. In these parents' minds there is no room for love, friendship, or respect for both. Like political fanatics, they split the world into good and evil. "Agree with me," they announce, "or be my enemy." Under these circumstances, it is not unusual for family, friends, and even professionals to take sides. However, this kind of "support" is rarely helpful. Rather, it simply means more soldiers on the field and more casualties in the war.

If you stop and think about it, you will realize that the most powerful supporter you can gain is your ex-spouse. If, over time, you can show him or her that you want nothing more than is fair, that you will accept nothing less, and that you insist on a fair process, then you will have won over a truly powerful ally.

The Power of Reward and Punishment

To whatever extent someone believes that you control something important to him or her, you can reward or punish that person by dispensing or witholding what you have, or by threatening to do so. The obvious things over which you may have at least some control in a divorce are a house, other possessions, money, and access to the children, now or in the future. Less tangible, but no less important resources are respect, recognition, communication, understanding, caring, cooperation, independence, and support as a parent.

When there are substantial differences between people, constructive negotiation almost always requires that both parties realize that the other can help them or hurt them. Why bother to negotiate if you think the other person can do nothing that really matters to you? In practice, however, reward and punishment have very different effects. Rewarding—saying and showing that you can and will help the other person meet their needs in exchange for help in meeting yours—may work slowly, but almost always works in the direction of a win-win agreement. Punishment, whether in the form of criticism, threats, withholding of financial support, or blocking of access to the children, may force a degree of compliance, but almost always at the cost of greater enmity.

It is important to realize that power does not come from always being rewarding or from always being punitive. If you give away what you have by agreeing to any and all of your ex-spouse's demands without getting anything in return, you will have little or no power left when you need it. If you do nothing but coerce, demand, threaten, and take, sooner or later your victim will find a way to victimize you. However, if you consistently work toward and reward cooperation, and if you consistently refuse to be moved by threats or punishment, then you will gain power and see that it can be used constructively.

The Power of Detachment and Self-control

A young woman tells her friend that eighteen months after she left him, her ex-husband can still ruin her day with a hostile comment, ruin her week with a threat. She has never gotten over her need for his approval and her fear of his anger. He still has the power to reward her with his ever-so-rare praise, to punish her with his easily provoked criticism, to terrify her with his threats. Until she detaches her self-esteem from his judgment, finds ways not to be upset by his condemnation, refuses to be intimidated by his threats, she will be unable to stand up for her own or her children's needs adequately.

A man who is trying hard to reach a sensible custody agreement with his still-angry and vindictive ex-wife finds himself losing his temper, yelling and screaming, whenever she accuses him of "deserting" the children by leaving her. Until he finds a way to hear her provocative accusations as signs of her own hurt and desperation rather than proof of his guilt, he will not be able to work with her in the children's interest or his own.

There is no easy way to gain detachment, to grow in self-control. However, two approaches can help. One is to find other sources of support for your self-esteem. If people you respect know and value you as a good parent and a worthy person, then condemnation from your ex-spouse becomes much less important. The second is simply to ask yourself "So what?" "So what if he thinks I'm a bad parent?" "So what if she treats me like a deserter?" "So what if he refuses to pay support?" By asking this question again and again, you may poke a hole through your fear, your anger, your neediness, and find that the true answer is, "I can live with that."

The Power of Small Steps

Not long ago two psychologists carried out an experiment. They went to half the houses in a neighborhood and asked if the owners would be willing to sign a petition in favor of safe driving. Most of those who were asked agreed. A month later different representatives went to every house in the neighborhood asking to put up large, ugly signs saying, "Drive Carefully." As you might expect, very few of the homeowners who had never been approached before agreed to let their lawns be used in this way. However, more than half of the people who had taken the tiny step of signing a petition were now willing to take the much larger step of putting a large sign in their front yards. The experimenters reasoned that the small step of signing a petition had led those homeowners to see themselves as good, civic-minded citizens. With that self-image to live up to, the large signs did not seem so farfetched. Superman may leap tall buildings in a single bound, but most of us get where we are going much as these psychologists did, by taking a lot of small steps.

Time after time I have seen divorcing parents start out literally miles apart, but reach a fair and workable agreement through months and sometimes years of patient, painstaking work. One parent takes the risk of leaving rather than continuing in a dying relationship. The other is hurt and angry, but finds inner and outer resources that gradually help. The children are upset; behavioral and school problems emerge. At first the parents blame each other, but they both talk to and work with the children. The first legal papers arrive and create panic, but communication and responsiveness eventually clear the air. They try to work things out together, but get into terrible arguments. They agree to see a mediator. After many hours of tears and hard work, they reach an agreement. A year later it needs change, but the trust they gained in their mediation makes it easier. The children get on about the business of growing up; the parents begin to build separate, better lives.

The Power of Transformation

It is naive to assume that if you negotiate in a fair and principled way, your ex-spouse will automatically do the same. It is more likely, at least at first, that your principled approach will be misunderstood as softness or weakness. Your calm may be met by anger. Your attempts to separate your personal feelings for each other from the problem of rearing the children may be met by even more strident personal attacks. Your proposal, "Let's agree on a fair way to figure this out," may be met by, "Sure, my way." Don't give up or be provoked into retaliation. Rather, use your strength to transform win-lose into win-win thinking.

Your ex-spouse threatens: "If you don't agree today, I'll be in court tomorrow."

A transforming response: "I can't allow myself to make such important decisions under that kind of pressure. Let's agree on a reasonable time span to finalize our talks."

Your ex-spouse manipulates: "Yeah, the support check is late, and it's going to be even later until I start seeing the kids when I want to."

Your response: "It's bad for the kids when we treat them as bargaining chips. Can we agree that we'll deal with their issues based on their needs, and our money issues separately?"

It does not take much strength or power to threaten or to exchange manipulations and blows. It does take a great deal of strength to cling to your goal of a solution that works for everyone, whatever the provocations. To the extent that you simply refuse to be manipulated or threatened, you have gained solid ground on which to stand. When you can consistently transform threats into productive give-and-take, you become truly powerful.

The Power of Persuasion

It does not hurt to try to convince your ex-spouse that your view is the correct one. Ultimately, persuading others means convincing them that your ideas will meet their needs. Or, as Lee Iacocca puts it, "I never made a deal with any lasting value unless the other guy felt he'd won too." If one argument does not work, try a different one.

Of course, a major part of persuasion is listening. How else can you learn what is important to the person you are dealing with? But if you listen, really listen, you take the risk that your ex-spouse may persuade you. It sometimes helps to remember that once in a long while, the other person may be right. Perhaps the offer that he or she just made is the winning solution for all of you.

The Subject Is Cooperation

Once you and your ex-spouse are motivated to negotiate, the next step is not deciding what to talk about, but rather how to proceed. The time and energy you invest at the start, working together to create a context for cooperation, will be repaid many times over as you continue. Think about this idea: "My ex-spouse and I are working together to resolve our mutual problems." This attitude is what I mean by a context for cooperation. It is the two of you together against the hurt, the financial strains, the confusion stemming from your divorce, not two people against each other.

There are three important ingredients of a fair process: equal power, equal access to information, and some kind of objective standards. Without these elements, whatever solutions you reach are likely to be lopsided, inadequate, unworkable, or unfair. When these three ingredients are present, both the agreement you eventually reach and the way you get there promise to be realistic and fair.

Managing Your Feelings

Divorce brings people face-to-face with basic issues, often for the first time. Negotiations usually stir up strong feelings. At first, divorcing parents may be afraid even to be in the same room. As they talk, frustration, anger, guilt, and fear are nearly inevitable. Sometimes sadness and tenderness reappear, and can feel just as threatening. It is terribly tempting to end negotiations when strong feelings flare up. It is vitally important to keep the talks alive.

Parents who work out their problems successfully point to several approaches that helped them.

1. Save your strongest feelings for somewhere else. Kick a tree or scream while you are alone in your car. Better yet, find a friend or therapist with whom you can be honest, who can help you ride the waves of your feelings with no harm done.

2. Give yourself time. Count to ten, take a break, give yourself enough time to process your feelings. Slow things down. A minute, an hour, or a day later, the sense of what was said may emerge from the smoke and fire of your emotions. Your response can be many things—determined, firm, understanding, transforming, but it does not need to add fuel to the fire.

3. Express your feelings nondestructively. Use the ideas pre-

sented in Chapter 5 to get your feelings across in ways that minimize their damage and maximize your chance of being listened to rather than reacted to.

4. Use your feelings. I have often seen anger or sorrow break a deadlock. Strong feelings have clout. When they are powerful, genuine, and honestly expressed, they can break down long-standing barriers. When you feel like attacking, ask yourself if the real feeling is not vulnerability. When you flare into anger, ask if your hidden feeling is not guilt or sorrow. When you are most tempted to strike out at your ex-spouse, look at him or her through the eyes of your children.

One couple mediated with me for months. They had worked out most of their issues, but whenever they got close to an agreement, the woman would stall or make a new demand. I suspected that she was trying to hold on to the last threads of the relationship with her ex-husband. I might have been able to help them past this stage by making her aware of her stalling. Her ex-husband, however, solved the problem much more directly. He finally got mad, really mad. He did not "blow up" or stalk out. He became righteously angry at her and showed it. She could not help but feel the force and genuineness of his feelings.

Surprisingly, they finalized their agreement that same day. Did he browbeat her into signing? Not at all. I think that his genuine anger accomplished two things—it let her know that he was really serious, someone who really had to be reckoned with, and perhaps more important, it met her need for him to relate to her honestly.

Moving Ahead

Once the two of you have agreed to negotiate, and negotiate fairly, half the battle is won. The next crucial step is to identify issues and interests of concern that you can discuss without becoming trapped in nonnegotiable positions. Legitimate issues include, but are not limited to, the following:

1. The eventual legal definition of child custody.
2. How everyday and major decisions about the children will be made.

3. The amount of time the children will spend with each parent.
4. The kinds of time the children will spend with each parent—overnights, everyday activities, recreation.
5. How that time will be scheduled.
6. How and when property will be divided.
7. Child support.
8. Spousal support.

It is tempting to take absolute positions. After all, they seem to be accurate expressions of your strong feelings, and that is how most of us have learned to bargain:

"There's no way you can ever have custody of the children."

"You're crazy if you think you can get part of my business."

"I'll never share custody with you."

"I'm going to make sure you don't get one penny of support."

"The kids will live with me, that's all there is to it."

"You'll never get me out of the house."

"I'll quit my job before I'll support you."

Once you have taken this kind of position, you can do little more than defend it; similarly, your ex-spouse has few options but to attack it. Perhaps you will be able to soften or give up your stance in exchange for a meaningful softening or retreat from your ex-spouse's equally defended position. It is more likely that the two of you will end up like two feuding neighbors, hurling insults over a wall of mistrust and anger.

Compare these fortified positions with clear advocacy of your underlying *interests*:

"I want the children to feel secure. How can we do that?"

"It's really important that I continue to feel that I'm in control of how hard I work at my business. I'd hate to feel like a slave to you or the court."

"I don't want either of us to feel desperate for money."

"Right now our home is a very important source of stability for me and the kids."

"The kids are still the central part of my life. I want to spend as much time with them as I can."

Even when you have worked out most of the issues, sometimes a difference of positions on even a minor question may come to seem insurmountable. One couple had solved all of their property, support, and custody issues but one. The mother wanted her ex-husband to provide transportation in both directions when their daughter was transferred from one parent's home to the other. He felt this request was unfair and unacceptable. Their stubborn defense of these positions eventually destroyed all the work they had done. How much easier it would have been if each of them could have voiced their interests and values:

Laura: My car isn't reliable any more. Knowing how upset you get whenever I mess up your schedule, I am afraid I'd be late and we'd end up in an argument.

Sam: You're right. It is very important to me that you be reliable about schedules. But it just doesn't feel fair for me to drive both ways.

Laura: What about it makes it seem unfair to you? The extra cost?

Sam: No, it's not the money, it's the time. I'd end up spending nearly two hours on the freeway with Allison. That's too big a chunk of my time with her.

Laura: How would you feel if we could make up that time with her—maybe with an extra weekend day once a month?

Sam: I guess I could live with that.

Keep Your Options Open

Picture yourself and your ex-spouse in a complex and dangerous game, not against each other, but against a hostile and implacable foe, an enemy who wants to take your money, hurt your children, and embitter your lives. With each move, this clever and powerful opponent drains your resources, limits your choices, cuts off your options, forces you into a corner. He would like nothing more than to see both of you without emotional or financial support, isolated from friends and family, unable to communicate with each other, and working at cross-purposes. When you have no choice but to defend one limited position, separated from your equally isolated ex-spouse by a chasm of distrust and frustration, your common enemy will have little trouble winning this nightmarish game.

Viewed in this way, your strategy seems obvious. Band together with your ex-spouse against this common foe. Keep your communication lines open, ready to compare notes and agree on each step as needed. Keep your options open—perhaps during this period the children will be more secure in your home; perhaps the reverse will be true down the road. Right now it might make sense to invest more than you would like in your ex-spouse's support, giving him or her a chance to reenter the job market at a higher level. That might give the two of you some much-needed maneuvering room later on. Keeping your joint options open gives the two of you the edge against the enemies you both face: fear, frustration, confusion, loss, and rage.

Principled negotiation, with or without the help of attorneys or a mediator, means transforming destructive conflict into a cooperative search for a fair and realistic solution. Few divorcing parents find it easy, but equally few find it impossible. It remains the most efficient and least destructive way for parents to build an agreement that works well for both of them and their children.

CHAPTER 9

Making It Legal

Success or failure for a divorcing family depends much more on how the parents manage their feelings, conflicts, and responsibilties than on what their legal documents say. However, since divorce, like marriage, is a legal entity, a divorcing couple has no choice but to work within the judicial system. For divorcing parents, involvement with the law has two goals: to finalize the legal and financial aspects of the marital relationship, and to define and stabilize a new relationship that will best serve the children.

In simplest form, these goals are reached through a divorce decree or marital settlement agreement. This is a legal document usually written by parents or their attorneys, then ordered or approved by a judge. A complete settlement, or parenting, agreement specifies the division of assets and debts, spousal support, and tax matters, along with decisions concerning parenting. As the sample agreement later in this chapter shows, the parenting agreement may include a clause about the end of the marriage, a statement of values and goals, a definition of legal custody, and specific agreements about residences, timesharing (including holidays and vacations), parenting responsibilities and cooperation, and child support. It may also place restrictions on geographical moves or plan in other ways for changes in circumstances, such as specifying ways of resolving any future disputes.

Soon after deciding to divorce, parents have an extremely important choice to make. They need to determine which ways of working towards a marital settlement they will use. Most people end up using several different approaches simultaneously or one after the other.

Some parents rely primarily on the traditional method of using separate attorneys who, depending on their preferences, may provide information, advice, and guidance; facilitate or control communication between the parents; negotiate on the parent's behalf; and prepare for and undertake litigation. Other parents take a second approach, attempting to minimize their contact with lawyers by communicating and negotiating on their own, using books or legal service agencies as a source of forms and procedures, and, in effect, acting as their own attorneys. Still, other parents take a third approach, using private or court-sponsored mediators or conciliators to help them through the process. Parents doing their own negotiation or working through a mediator are well advised to have independent attorneys evaluate and ratify their negotiated agreement. Parents using any of these approaches may call upon experts to help with specific problems—for example, evaluating possessions, investments, or businesses; figuring out tax consequences; or evaluating a child's developmental level, strengths, and special needs.

If you have not already filled it out, this would be a good point to complete the checklist in Appendix I. It will help you assess the resources and limitations you and your ex-spouse are bringing to this process. It can help you determine whether or not you are ready to negotiate a custody agreement on your own, have a good chance of working out a mediated solution, or need more extensive legal or professional help.

The Do-It-Yourself Plan

The best agreement is one that is reached amicably by divorcing parents themselves. Whenever two parents are able to work out their differences with relatively little conflict, they and their children benefit. Parents rightfully feel better about themselves because of accomplishing a vital and difficult task, and gain security in knowing that both of them are motivated to follow the agreement. Since the children's well-being depends so directly on their parents' ability to work together and support each other as parents, a practical agreement negotiated in this way bodes well for their future. In many states, books are available detailing the legal steps and forms involved in a divorce. Appendix V lists several of these under the heading "Legal Matters." Although not all of the people who have used these books have successfully finalized their own divorces, it is a workable approach for many.

Nevertheless, it is important not to underestimate the difficulties involved in creating a successful parenting plan on your own. A wide variety of practical, financial, and legal issues all need to be negotiated realistically and with foresight, at a time when your personal resources may be strained, emotions are running high, and your relationship with your ex-spouse is at best changing dramatically. Parents often work hard to put together an agreement, only to be disappointed when they bring it to an attorney who tells them that they have failed to consider many crucial issues. Many parents will want or need more help than the "do-it-yourself" approach provides.

Mediation: The Best Approach for Many

Mediation is a highly desirable choice for couples with low or moderate levels of disagreement and conflict. I have also seen it work well for many high-conflict couples, especially when the parents are highly motivated to stay in mediation, and often after other approaches have failed or made things worse. In a recent study, psychologist Joan Kelly compared more than 400 divorcing parents, half of whom used mediation rather than the adversarial legal process. On every measure, including fairness, custody and visitation arrangements, spousal support, and division of property, both men and women rated mediation equal to or better than litigation.

Effective mediation helps to build trust where it is lacking, and uncovers shared values that make negotiation and compromise possible. You should not rule out mediation simply because you lack trust for your ex-spouse, feel that the two of you cannot communicate, or have strongly held differences on vital issues. The more important the issues are to both of you, the more motivation is available to empower your search for a solution.

An attorney-mediator or a mediation team composed of an

attorney and a mental health specialist can help in many ways. Mediation:

1. provides a powerful structure for problem solving and dispute resolution.
2. teaches and models a fair and nondestructive approach.
3. clarifies legal and financial issues.
4. helps identify areas where expert input is needed.
5. improves communication and communication skills.
6. separates problems from personalities.
7. helps deal with strong feelings and relationship issues.
8. encourages the exploration of alternatives and options.
9. moves parents towards resolution and agreement.
10. produces parenting and property agreements that are in legally acceptable form and are respected by most courts.

In many cases, mediation can guide a couple to a successful divorce and custody agreement more quickly and less expensively than using lawyers to negotiate and litigate.

Mediation means taking responsibility for both the method and the outcome of your dispute. You take charge of the process in the act of choosing mediation rather than, for example, adversarial litigation. To be in equal control of the outcome, you need to become the expert on your own situation. Since you have chosen to keep the reins in your hands, it will no longer do to let someone else tell you what is right or wrong for you.

In financial terms, such independence means knowing and understanding the facts about your own and your ex-spouse's finances. You will need to know or be able to figure out

1. your own and your ex-spouse's current income and expenses.
2. your own and your ex-spouse's anticipated future income and expenses.
3. reasonable household budgets under different custody plans.

4. the nature and value of the financial assets from your marriage—house, cars, furniture, investments, pensions, business assets, etc.

Much of this information can and will be developed in the course of mediation. However, the more clearly you understand your own and your ex-spouse's present and predictable financial situations, the better able you will be to generate and evaluate options, negotiate effectively, and determine what is fair and workable. A mediator should be able to provide you with forms to help you gather and organize this financial information.

In terms of parenting, other information is important:

1. What are the children's needs based on their ages and developmental levels?
2. Do the children have any special needs, for example an unusual requirement for stability, a special diet or medical regimen, access to special educational programs, counseling, or medical care?
3. Do the children have strong preferences that need to be considered—for example, to remain in the family home, to stay close to friends, to a particular school, or to spend significantly more time with one parent?
4. What is the meaning of the children's preferences? Based on the children's age and maturity, are their preferences meaningful and realistic?
5. What are the implications of the children's preferences? How will the children react if we decide to go against their desires?
6. Given predictable income levels, careers, geographic location, access to transportation, child care, schools, etc., what custody and time-sharing options are possible? Which would work best for the children? Which would work best for the adults?

Choosing a Mediator

If you decide to mediate, it is important to find a highly qualified, experienced, and impartial mediator with whom you and your ex-spouse can work comfortably. It makes sense to "shop around," getting the names of several potential mediators, talking to all of them, and choosing the best.

Mediation can be a powerful process, but it cannot work instantaneously. Before entering mediation, consider how much time, energy, and attention you are willing to invest in this approach towards a mutually beneficial resolution.

Finding a Mediator

A variety of potential sources for referrals to qualified mediators are available:
 1. your local domestic or family court.
 2. your local or state bar association.
 3. attorneys whom you know or with whom you have worked.
 4. therapists or family physicians with whom you have worked.
 5. your church.
 6. listings in the yellow pages under mediation services, attorneys, psychologists, and marriage or family counselors.
 7. other divorcing or divorced parents.
 8. local support groups for divorcing parents.
 9. your county department of social services.
10. your local family service agency.

Questions to Ask Potential Mediators

Here are some questions to ask each potential mediator.
 1. What percentage of your work involves mediation?
 2. What percentage of your work involves divorce mediation?
 3. Do you usually mediate both financial and child custody issues?
 4. What is your professional background?
 5. What degrees and licenses do you hold?
 6. What specific training have you had in divorce mediation?

7. How long have you worked with divorcing couples?
8. Do you belong to a professional organization for mediators?
9. How many divorce mediations have you completed?
10. What family members would you want to see?
11. For children the ages of ours, what do you think about shared custody? Noncustodial mothers? Primary-parent fathers? (Ask about any other key issues in your situation.)
12. How much do you charge?
13. How long would you expect to work with us?
14. What is the expected cost for the mediation?

Evaluating Your Attorney

Much of Chapter 4 was devoted to a discussion of when lawyers are needed, how to find and select a lawyer who will really help you, and how to work with your attorney constructively. If you are at the point of choosing an attorney or are already working with one, it may be useful for you to review that chapter.

As your case progresses, you will have many chances to evaluate your attorney. What is the quality of your relationship with him or her? Has your attorney consistently been available to you, devoted adequate and timely attention to your case, informed you when information was needed, counseled you when guidance was needed, listened to you when you voiced your own and your children's needs? Has he or she established a working relationship with the other attorney, or have their battles been superimposed on yours? Have necessary steps such as discovery and pleadings been handled promptly, professionally, and with restraint, or in a careless, provocative, or incendiary manner? Is your case moving forward or backward? Remember, you hired the attorney, and can replace him or her if you need to.

The Goal: A Successful Child Custody Agreement

The following agreement was reached by Kate and Richard Nash (not their real names) through negotiation and mediation over the course of several months. Their attorney-mediator wrote the document based on input from both parents. Each parent had a separate attorney who then reviewed a draft of the agreement. This review led to a few relatively minor changes, but left the core of their agreement intact.

Remember that the format for this kind of agreement may vary from state to state or jurisdiction to jurisdiction, and that a complete marital settlement agreement would define property and financial matters along with child custody issues. Every couple has different needs. This agreement worked for Kate and Richard; it is not meant as a model for any other couple.

STIPULATED PARENTING AGREEMENT*
RECITALS

We, Richard Nash, here referred to as Father, and Katherine Nash, here referred to as Mother, are husband and wife. We have one child from our marriage, Matthew, seven years old.

Because of irreconcilable differences, we have separated and filed a petition for the dissolution of our marriage.

INTENT

Each of us has been deeply involved in a responsible and nurturing parental relationship with Matthew since his birth. Each of us considers himself/herself a fit parent, and respects the other as a fit parent as well. We both recognize the importance to Matthew of maintaining his relationship with each of us.

Although resolved to the dissolution of our marriage, our primary concern continues to be Matthew's best interest. We are seeking joint custody of Matthew since it best reflects the sharing of parental rights and duties that has been the case since Matthew's birth and during our separation.

Each of us wishes to continue to participate fully in all major

---

*Derived in part from Jay Folberg, ed., *Joint Custody and Shared Parenting* (Washington, D.C.: The Bureau of National Affairs, Inc., 1984), Appendix B.

decisions concerning Matthew. Except for the duties and obligations imposed and assumed under this agreement, each of us wishes to be free from interference and control of the other, and respects that wish in the other.

AGREEMENT
PARENTING

I. Mother and Father will share joint legal custody and physical parenting of Matthew. Matthew's parenting shall be shared as stipulated below.

PLACES OF RESIDENCE

2. (a) During his school year, commencing with the Sunday before the first day of school and ending with the Sunday following the last day of school, Matthew shall live with each parent for one week at a time, alternating between them every Sunday at 5:00 P.M. During his summer vacation, he shall live with each parent for two consecutive weeks at a time, alternating between them every second Sunday at 5:00 P.M. This residential agreement is subject to the provisions of paragraph 11 concerning changes in circumstances.

(b) For the purposes of this agreement, the schedule of residency described above shall be considered to have started with Matthew's stay with Father during the first week of school, September _____ through _____, _____.

VACATIONS, HOLIDAYS, AND SPECIAL TIMES

3. Matthew will spend holidays and vacations in the care of the parent he is regularly scheduled to be with, except for the following:

Matthew's birthday: with Mother in even-numbered years, with Father in odd-numbered years

Mother's Day: with Mother

Father's Day: with Father

In even-numbered years:

The first half of Matthew's Christmas holiday, not to include Christmas Day—with Father

Christmas Day through the end of Matthew's Christmas vacation—with Mother

9:00 A.M. Thanksgiving Day through Thanksgiving
Night—with Father

In odd-numbered years:

The first half of Matthew's Christmas holiday, not to
include Christmas Day—with Mother

Christmas Day through the end of Matthew's Christmas
vacation—with Father

9:00 A.M. Thanksgiving Day through Thanksgiving
Night—with Mother

SHARING AND DIVISION OF
PARENTAL RESPONSIBILITIES

4. (a) The parent with whom Matthew is living shall be responsible for his care, transportation, and for any emergency decisions concerning his health or welfare. Each parent shall be empowered to obtain emergency health care for Matthew without the consent of the other parent.

(b) Both parents shall consult and agree on all major decisions concerning Matthew. These include but are not limited to his general welfare, education, religious affiliation and upbringing, and nonemergency medical and mental-health care.

(c) Both parents agree to confer as needed concerning Matthew's needs and development, and to share and make accessible all of Matthew's school, medical, dental, and other pertinent records, including but not limited to report cards, vacation schedules, class programs, results of standardized or diagnostic tests, order forms for school pictures, and all communications from health-care providers.

(d) Both agree to notify the other in advance of important events concerning Matthew, including but not limited to school meetings and public events in which Matthew will participate.

(e) Both parents agree to notify the other parent of any illness requiring medical attention or any emergency involving Matthew as soon as reasonably possible.

(f) Both parents value and agree to support flexibility in adjusting schedules and responsibilities to meet changing needs and circumstances. The specific terms of this agreement are to be interpreted liberally to give Matthew the maximum benefit of both parents' love and care.

(g) It is mutually understood and agreed that these schedules and responsibilities are subject to modification by mutual agreement in accordance with paragraph 7.

(h) In accepting the broad grant of privileges and responsibilities confirmed by this joint custodial agreement, both parents specifically agree that they will not use such privileges and responsibilities to frustrate, deny, or control the relationship between Matthew and the other parent. Both parents agree to work cooperatively in future planning consistent with Matthew's best interests and in amicably resolving any disputes that may arise with respect to his upbringing.

CHANGE OF RESIDENCE

5. (a) Recognizing that the benefits to Matthew of shared parenting could be threatened by geographical separation, we agree that neither parent will move Matthew's place of residence out of the County of _____ without the written consent of the other parent or a court order.

(b) If either parent intends to move his or her residence outside of the State of _____, he or she shall provide the other parent with sixty (60) days advance notice in writing of that intention.

CHILD SUPPORT

(NOTE: detailed provisions specifying each parent's responsibilites for ordinary child support, nonordinary costs, health insurance, life insurance, trusts, annuities, dependency exemptions, etc., can go here.)

CHANGES IN CIRCUMSTANCES

7. If circumstances change in such a way as to affect materially the care of Matthew or his contacts with either parent, the residential, scheduling, and other provisions of this agreement shall be reconsidered by the parents.

(a) If either parent changes residence outside of the County of _____ , or if either parent changes job or career responsibilities in a manner that affects Matthew's care, his parents will attempt to modify aspects of the then-existing agreement to ensure the continuation of shared custody, jointly choosing a parenting plan that will meet Matthew's developmental and individual needs while providing him with access to both parents in roughly equal amounts.

(b) In making career and residential choices in the future, both parents shall consider Matthew's needs and preferences along with facilitation of this shared parenting plan.

AMENDMENTS

8. If Mother and Father agree upon modifications of this agreement which significantly affect this shared parenting plan, or are meant to be permanent, they shall be added to this agreement in writing, and the revised agreement filed with the court.

DISPUTE RESOLUTION

9. Should disputes arise concerning Matthew's parenting, both parents agree to work together sincerely to resolve them in Matthew's best interest. Should the parents be unable to resolve such disputes through their own efforts, at the request of either parent they shall use the process of mediation with a mediator on whom they mutually agree. If they can not agree on a private mediator, they shall use the Family Court Services. Both parents agree to remain in the mediation process to its conclusion prior to either parent's initiating litigation relating to this agreement.

DEATH OF ONE OR BOTH PARENTS

10. Should either parent die before Matthew reaches the age of majority, the surviving parent shall assume full custody and care of Matthew.

BINDING EFFECT

11. Both parents agree that this agreement is a complete and final settlement of their custody and child-support rights stemming from their marriage. We expressly release each other from any current or future obligations and payments arising from such custody and child-support rights other than those stipulated in this agreement. This agreement is expressly made binding upon the heirs, assigns, executors, administrators, representatives, and successors of both parents.

12. Both parents agree that this agreement will be submitted to

the court for approval, and may be incorporated into any decree that may be entered in the dissolution of our marriage.

IN WITNESS WHEREOF, the parties have signed their names.

Richard Nash, Respondent	Katherine Nash, Petitioner
Attorney for Respondent	Attorney for Petitioner

When Katherine and Richard submitted this agreement to the court, the judge incorporated it into their final divorce decree without changes. In most jurisdictions, an agreement of this kind, worded to reflect your joint intent, reviewed and subject to the advice of your individual attorneys, and prepared in the format used in your jurisdiction, can readily be submitted to the court. This is a custody agreement only; a complete marital settlement agreement would also specify spousal support and property issues. Those financial issues can be separated from the custody agreement, so your parenting agreement can be approved by the court before or after those other matters.

The way in which the custody of a child is defined can affect two other thorny issues—dependency exemptions, and the question of which parent, if either, stays in the former family home. These are areas where parents, even if they agree, need to obtain legal advice.

It is important to recognize that some of the provisions of this kind of custody agreement, for example section 7 (a), are not strictly enforceable by the court; they are important because they set the tone for the future by stating clearly how the parents intend to proceed. Statements of values and intentions can remain general. However, it is usually best to be precise about other areas, particularly the times when a child will be with each parent.

Many parents are able to negotiate or mediate the terms of their marital settlement without going to court as adversaries. There is no doubt that those parents and their children are real winners—they have the satisfaction of solving their own problems rather than having to rely on "imperfect strangers" to impose a settlement on them. They and their children can feel secure in the knowledge that their agreement was built by the same hands and hearts that brought the children into the world.

But What If We Go to Court?

Even if your case goes to court, the principles presented in this book still apply. Most judges are far more impressed by fact than argument. They diligently look for the gems of truth in the midst of inflammatory words. They have learned to tell the difference between a parent selfishly bent on attack and defense, and one determined to advocate for the child first and his or her own interests second.

I remember watching a very principled attorney in court, up against an advocate with a reputation for distortions and "dirty tricks." The win-lose lawyer went on for a long time, waving his hands, playing fast and loose with the facts, painting his client as a saint and smearing the other parent in every way he could. I saw the hurt and anger in the parent being attacked, and the restraint it took for the win-win attorney not to strike back in kind. However, when it was her turn to speak, she said a few calm, clear words focusing on the facts and on the children's basic needs. She took five minutes where the other lawyer had taken twenty, and relied on good sense and problem solving, not on personal attack.

While we waited in the corridor for the judge's decision, I asked her how she had kept from responding to the other attorney's hostility, sarcasm, and half-truths. "It used to be hard," she said with a bit of a smile, "but once I realized that I win nine out of ten decisions when he's opposing me, it made it a whole lot easier."

CHAPTER 10

Rebuilding

Once you have made it through the "crazies"—the high-stress, topsy-turvy time before and after your separation, it is time to start rebuilding. Like a city after an earthquake, your new life will never be same as it was. Some old and treasured parts may have been damaged beyond repair. However, the upheaval may also have cleared areas where beautiful new structures can grow.

A New Relationship

Getting on with your life requires a crucial transformation: your old intimate-but-unworkable relationship with your ex-spouse must change into a more distant, but working alliance. As long as you have not been able to let go of the feelings, good and bad, that held the two of you together *and* pushed you apart, your new life can only struggle to grow around the edges of that old relationship.

As discussed in Chapter 5, Constance Ahrons studied 98 normal families in Wisconsin as they tried to make this vital transition. Just about half of the couples, she found, emerged from the chaotic early years of divorce successfully—as what she came to call "cooperative colleagues" or "perfect pals." The cooperative colleagues made up more than one-third of the total, perfect pals the remainder.

If you and your ex-spouse fall in the perfect pal category, you find it remarkably easy to get along. Well past the differences that split you up as a couple, you have no difficulty making cooperative plans or even spending time together. You might, for example, plan a joint birthday party for your child, or call to share some happy news. Many of the perfect pals among

Ahrons' parents were strongly child centered; joint custody usually matched their needs and abilities well.

Despite all we hear about feuding parents, the largest group in Ahrons' study were cooperative colleagues—divorced parents who had put their old animosities aside to the point of being able to work together and support each other as parents. Unlike perfect pals, they were not likely to share a child's birthday or call each other just to talk. They did, however, interact well enough to minimize potential conflicts and cooperate concerning their children. They and their children did well with a variety of custody plans.

However, nearly half of the parents in her study were not so fortunate. Five years after divorce, they were still unhappily or angrily involved with each other. "Angry associates" made up 25 percent of the group. They had moderate amounts of contact with each other but were often unable to cooperate—the old, angry feelings from their marriages were too strong to allow new, more businesslike patterns to take root. About the same number had turned into "fiery foes"—five years of separation had not cooled their fury. These parents, because of their clashes, had as little contact with each other as possible. When they did meet or talk, they fought. Predictably, these couples were unable to agree or cooperate about their children, making any custody arrangement unstable and fraught with problems.

Even the angriest of these parents seemed to sense that their lives and the lives of their children would be better if they could learn to get along better. Almost all the parents Ahrons talked to wished to be on better terms with their former spouse. Hardly any of these ex-partners, cooperative or feuding, wished to get back together, but many hoped for less bitterness between themselves, and for more open and frequent communication concerning their children.

Formulas for Transformation

The first tool for freeing oneself from the destructive hold of an old relationship is recognizing and accepting what has been lost. Many people fail or refuse to accept the fact that their marriage, and all that it meant to them, really is over. Instead they unconsciously try to continue the marriage through animosity and fighting.

Every so often newspapers carry a story about someone who keeps the corpse of a loved one, sometimes for years. It is easy to see this behavior as a bizarre aberration, yet we tend to view as normal the equally strange and often more destructive forms of negative intimacy that develop when one or both spouses cannot let go. Their anger animates the corpse of a dead marriage long after it should have been laid to rest. Only by recognizing and accepting your losses can you be free to go on.

Those losses are not limited to the closeness, warmth, support, and love you once shared, nor even to the vital roles you played in each other's lives. Often the hardest things to let go of are the least tangible—dreams of a special kind of family life, a deep image of oneself as a terrific husband, wife, or parent, a yearning for the passionate love you may have shared for a while, for the larger-than-life feelings that were once so strong, for the hopes and dreams of young lovers.

"I was too scared to let go," Joan says. "If I let myself think the marriage had failed, I felt totally panicked. My whole picture of myself was as a wife and mother. Giving that up felt like dying."

Admitting that it is over, finished, gone, ended once and for all, can be intensely painful. Fear of that pain keeps many chasing fantasies, trapped in futile attempts at reconciliation or the destructive rituals of hostile intimacy. Accepting the losses and the pain sets you free.

How Free Are You?
A Checklist for Identifying Old Entanglements

1. If I knew I would be meeting my ex-spouse five minutes from now, I would feel
   A. no different than I usually do.
   B. pleased, like meeting an old friend.
   C. excited or full of anticipation.
   D. angry or hostile.
   E. dreadful; I'd want to avoid it if I could.

2. When we talk about the children, we
   A. communicate in a businesslike way.
   B. talk pleasantly and easily about them and our-selves.
   C. often talk about old times or about our relation-ship.
   D. have trouble; we often get into an argument.
   E. would be fighting in a minute—it's impossible.
3. Why did the marriage break up?
   A. It was nobody's fault, or it was due to things both of us did or failed to do.
   B. He or she pushed it over the edge, but I am aware of things I did or failed to do that contributed to it.
   C. It was a mistake; we should be back together.
   D. He or she was impossible to live with; I had no choice.
   E. He or she is to blame; I have to pick up the pieces.
4. Right now issues and problems from our marriage or divorce
   A. take up only a small share of my time and energy.
   B. require attention, but are not interfering with other parts of my life.
   C. are very important and meaningful to me.
   D. occupy much of my time and energy; they keep me from doing other things.
   E. preoccupy me night and day; they crowd out almost all other needs.
5. The thought of a new relationship is
   A. positive; I am in one or ready for one.
   B. attractive; I am cautious and hold back, but I am moving in that direction.
   C. not attractive; I can't imagine having the feelings that I used to have with my ex-spouse.
   D. attractive, but I'd worry about how my current problems would affect it.
   E. something I can't handle right now; I'm too pre-occupied with divorce problems to handle it.

Interpretating Your Answers

If most of your answers were "A" or "B," you seem to be making good progress towards being a perfect pal or cooperative colleague. Keep up the good work!

If most of your answers were "C," you appear to retain strong positive feelings about your ex-spouse. You may still hope for reconciliation. If so, it is important to find out if that is realistic. If the relationship is really over, but you have not been able to let go, then it is time to accept that truth, mourn for what you have lost, and move on.

A preponderance of "D" and "E" responses indicates a continuing unhappy preoccupation with your marriage or divorce. The problems may be specific—financial, legal, personal, or centering on the children. If so, solving them efficiently needs to be at the top of your priority list. Or, the whole package of problems may be caused by not letting go, by continuing to live in the ruins of your old relationship rather than finding a new space and building a new life. Counseling may be the most efficient way to resolve your underlying feelings.

If we trust them, our natural reactions show us the way to recover. Everyone who has experienced loss recognizes the mournful flashbacks when a song or a place or a whiff of perfume reminds us of the past. These memories are gifts. We need not be afraid to relive them, but we must be sure not to live in them. Memory is like a river; if we dive in and swim across, we emerge cleansed and revitalized.

It Wasn't All Bad

Hand in hand with recognizing and accepting losses goes remembering and valuing what you gained. Your relationship was a rich mixture of experiences—things shared and things kept to yourself, special moments and hard times, fantasies and realities, familiar patterns and whole new ways of being. True, your relationship did not end the way you wanted it to, but should that be allowed to destroy everything of value from the very beginning?

Every time you allow yourself to recognize something that you learned, times when you grew in your previous relationship, you free yourself from the need to return to it or try to keep it alive. Everything you went through, everything you did or said, how you enjoyed the good times and how you dealt with the bad, all contributed to your own growth. Even the things you may regret about your marriage, the dishonesties, the distances, the hurts, the failures, can serve as powerful lessons for the future if you let them. Many people who successfully "let go" apply some version of the "equal-time rule": they make themselves spend as much time remembering the negative aspects of their marriage as the positive, their ex-spouse's strengths and weaknesses, and their own.

Don't Get Mad *or* Get Even—Get Ahead

It is easy, and sometimes accurate, to blame your ex-spouse for your troubles. When we are hurt, it seems to be a part of our reactions as humans to get mad and to want to get even. Although many divorcing people manage to get past this stage within a few years, like the cooperative colleagues and perfect pals mentioned previously, many do not. One factor that seems to ease the sting, decrease the pressure to hurt back, is personal success. Even the first stirrings of a new relationship can salve the wounds from the old. The give and take of a new friendship can help us feel worthwhile again. A child's progress can reaffirm our self-image as a good parent. Even something as small as listing one's own good points, learning to balance a checkbook, or cook a meal for the children can help mend self-confidence shattered by divorce.

One long-term investment that pays royal dividends for many divorcing people is career development. Especially for women who have been financially dependent because they have devoted themselves to home and family, going back to school, gaining new skills, and building a new career are powerful medicines. Some of the most frightened and dependent people I have worked with have been able to cut bonds that have limited them for years the day they got their first paycheck.

When her marriage broke up after twelve years, Marcia had to fight to get barely adequate support for herself and the children. Her attorney encouraged her to insist that the support continue long enough for her to return to school, complete her degree, and start her career. Rather than adding to her problems, the challenges of college were like a spring breeze to her. Each time I saw her, she looked and felt stronger and more sure of herself. She now earns a substantial income as an accountant—her chosen field—and thrives on the new-found stature her career provides.

Rolling Stones (Uphill)

If a person takes on a difficult task, one of two things is likely to happen. He or she may rise to the challenge, succeed, and have every right to feel proud, important, and accomplished. On the other hand, he or she may fail, accept the damages, and go on. But what happens if a person takes on an impossible job—something that, however important, simply cannot be accomplished? This kind of task has some major advantages. First, it offers permanent employment—no danger of working oneself out of the job. Second, the worker can stay busy and feel important endlessly. Some may point out that all that effort is futile, that this person has no chance of success. Our permanently busy and important person, however, simply smiles—after all, there is no chance of failure either.

One of the most frequent traps during and after marriage is the impossible task of changing someone else. Your ex-spouse may be alcoholic, overly controlling, violent, unreliable, manipulative, or simply different than you would like. If you accepted the job of changing him or her, you took on an impossible task. You may think you are doing it for the best of reasons, out of unselfish love and devotion, but it is likely that your real reasons are much more selfish—to be important and needed (to a damaged person), to prove how capable or long-suffering you are (at someone else's expense), to rescue (but rescuers always need victims).

The antidote is simple, but surprisingly hard to accept: give up trying to change your ex-spouse. This letting go does not mean giving up on your or your children's legitimate needs, or on working towards a more constructive relationship. But it does mean looking at and dealing with your ex-spouse "as is," without any expectation that he or she will ever change.

Paradoxically, your ex-spouse may surprise you by making some significant changes. It is not unusual for people to try new things and respond to their new situation following divorce. These departures from past behavior patterns can be a fertile source of resentments—for example, when a stingy ex-spouse supports a new mate in lavish style. But it is important to remind yourself that those changes have nothing to do with you. They were never under your control, and they are not meant to "show you" or "spite you."

Pillows and Pillars

The quality of our lives reflects the quality of our support systems. If you are lucky, you may already have plenty of what I call "pillows," those warm, supportive friends who help cushion our worst shocks, and enough "pillars" too—those equally necessary people whom we respect enough to listen to, and who care about us enough to let us know when we are off base. If so, they may already have helped you to survive the crash and encouraged you to get moving again.

However, you may not have enough pillows and pillars in your life. If you are shy or hesitant to make demands, you may have these potential supporters in your life but not realize who they are or be able to ask them for what you need. Go ahead and ask. Certainly divorce is a big enough crisis to justify reaching for support. Someone out there wants to help you, is willing to listen to you, will share your fears, your anger, and your tears. Someone sees the good qualities in you that you may have lost sight of, and will not be afraid to remind you of them. Who could help more than someone who has been through what you are going through? What about a group of such people? In almost every locality there are groups like Parents Without Partners that provide activities, services, and friendship for divorcing parents.

"Divorce," one parent said to me, "is when you find out who your real friends are." It is those real friends who can really help you to let go and move ahead.

Formulas for Transformation

1. **Recognize and accept your losses.** Think and act as though your marriage really is over. Discuss it with your children, your parents, and your friends. Use the natural mourning process to "dive in" but not live in the river of memories, both good and bad. Terminate periods of mourning with meaningful new activities.

2. **Recognize the good times and realize what you gained.** Don't dwell only on what you have lost. Examine your relationship from the start, looking at what you experienced for the first time, what challenges you met, what you learned.

3. **Don't get mad *or* get even—get ahead.** Refuse to throw any more energy or time than is absolutely necessary into the old relationship. Schedule businesslike communication about specific problems. Make plans. Invest yourself in new friendships, new involvements, education, career, etc.—build a new life.

4. **Don't push stones uphill; give up trying to change your ex-spouse.** Resolve to live your own life, not to improve, control, or change your ex-spouse. Deal with current, specific problems, not with your ex-spouse's character. Whenever you feel resentful because of something he or she has done or failed to do, put your feelings into steps toward independence rather than trying to change the other person.

5. **Find and benefit from your support system.** This is not a time to be shy or afraid of imposing on others. Find and use your real friends as pillows to cushion the hard times and as pillars to push you forward. Find groups of people who are going through, or who have already experienced, the problems you are facing.

A New Home

One of the biggest mistakes divorcing parents can make is to assume that one of them will stay in "the home" while the other goes away to live in something that is not a home. Of course, finances and practicality may dictate that one of the parents will continue to live in the family home for a period of time. Some children, particularly in the preschool years, may be very attached to the home they have known. However, it is vital for the parent who is leaving to create a new home as soon as possible.

Lack of money may limit what that home is. It may not be the detached, single-family dwelling of your dreams. However, it can be a real home nonetheless—a place that is yours, where you feel good, not a place where your children come to visit, but a place where they live when they are with you. Your home can be your territory, where, within reason, you get to determine the lifestyle and set the rules.

Experience has shown that both parents, however cooperative they are, feel a powerful need to determine how things are run in their own home. It really cannot be any other way; how we structure our space and time, when and what we eat, how seriously we take issues like bedtime, noise, tidiness, etc., flows from us as naturally as the way we walk or talk. A home, by definition, is where we can be ourselves, not where we follow someone else's rules.

Please notice, however, the phrase "within reason." I have seen many potentially good parenting arrangements break down because of patterns of behavior that no concerned parent, no matter how respectful of the other parent's rights, could tolerate. It is reasonable for each parent to determine his or her lifestyle, as long as that lifestyle is adequate for rearing healthy, well-adjusted children. It is not reasonable to raise children in a crash pad, a "home" centered around drug or alcohol abuse, or in a rapidly shifting series of unstable living arrangements or casual relationships.

I do not include among these unacceptable activities introducing children to a potential new mate. Children, especially younger ones, often benefit from the presence of an additional adult in their lives. The pain and difficulties of being a divorced single parent can be reduced enormously by a positive new relationship. One divorced parent does not have the right to try to force the other to be celibate or secretive about a new relationship "for the sake of the children."

However, I do include exposing the children to an endless stream of lovers. Casual affairs need to be treated as casual affairs. Children do not benefit by being expected to relate and adjust to a series of new "mommies" or "daddies." Until you are prepared to offer a meaningful relationship, and until a casual partner has demonstrated a meaningful degree of commitment to you and your children, he or she has little place in your home or your children's lives, particularly during their most vulnerable time—the first year after separation.

Everyday Disputes

Several issues come up again and again in custody disputes, problems concerning location of homes, acceptable foods, scheduling, children's friends and activities, school placement, supervision, clothes, toys, and discipline. When parents can communicate adequately, common sense can usually solve these problems. When parents continue to fight, common sense is the first casualty.

Location and Scheduling

Most professionals and cooperating parents agree that an ideal situation for a child of divorce is to have both parents living in the same neighborhood and close to the same school. Kenneth, a nine-year-old, is typical of these lucky children: "After school I can ride my bike to my Dad's place. He works at home so I can hang around there. Sometimes he lets me help him. Then when Mom gets done with work, I go there for dinner." Unlike many children of divorce, whose sense of helplessness and powerlessness often leads to depression, children in this fortunate situation can make choices about things that are important to them.

Many factors can make this degree of proximity impossible or less than desirable. Many parents who are sharing in the custody and care of their children end up living miles apart—

often in two different communities. Again, common sense and a degree of flexibility can lead to workable solutions. If the children are beyond infancy, longer stays with each parent may be workable, thus minimizing the number of transitions and the amount of transportation. If need be, one parent may take on the bulk of the transportation in exchange for some other considerations. Over the years a child may make friends in both neighborhoods.

Although less than ideal, when circumstances force parents to live hundreds or thousands of miles apart, there can still be a meaningful sharing of parenting. Clearly the children in these widely separated families cannot make frequent transitions. In many cases, it makes sense to designate one locale as home base for the school year, perhaps with the bulk of vacations and much of the summer at the other home. Some parents with older children have worked out year-by-year plans, although each child needs to be monitored closely to see if he or she is able to deal with such long periods away from a parent. Children from six to twelve years of age seem to do better with these changes than either very young children or teenagers. Pre-schoolers need more frequent contact with each parent, while teenagers have powerful needs to remain in a single school and to be involved with their chosen peer group.

If you or your ex-spouse have strong negative reactions to the thought of living in the same neighborhood, or if you find yourselves unable to come to a stable parenting agreement because of details of scheduling or transportation, issues that have little to do with your children are probably keeping you from working out commonsense solutions. If so, it is vital to figure out just what those underlying issues are in order to find ways of dealing with them.

Appendix II lists a variety of age-appropriate timesharing plans.

Junk Food

Although Wendy's and McDonald's are thriving, you would not believe it from what many divorcing parents claim. "Timmy is allergic to meat, milk, wheat, and chocolate," one father writes in a court declaration. "In addition, sugar or food additives make him hyperactive. While I, at considerable expense of time and effort, provide him an adequate diet completely free of these elements, his mother willfully refuses to recognize his special needs and consistently endangers his health."

Some children do have severe allergies to certain foods, molds, or dust. Their health can, and in some cases, has to be protected by limiting their exposure to these substances. The case for sugar and food additives causing or contributing to hyperactivity remains controversial. A few seriously hyperactive children do seem to do somewhat better when their diets are carefully controlled. However, the majority of children do not need special diets.

No doubt the diet of many families could be improved—more fiber and polyunsaturated fats, less cholesterol, sugar, and salt are frequently recommended. However, I meet infinitely more teenagers and young adults who are disturbed or damaged because their divorced parents were "hostility junkies" than those who have problems because of junk foods.

It is basically a matter of priorities. Children do need healthful food, but even more they need their intimate family world to be healthful. You and your ex-spouse create that world. Your mutual ability to define and stabilize that world is far more important in most cases than your child's need for a particular diet.

Special Schools

Much the same holds true for specialized educational placement. Many parents feel that their child will do much better in a particular private or religious school than in public school or any other educational setting. Some believe that this kind of change is vital to their child's educational progress and future. If two parents, divorced or otherwise, agree and can muster the resources to place or continue their child where they chose, no one will argue with them. However, when two divorced parents disagree strongly about school placement, destructive levels of hostility can easily arise.

Stan and Helen are a case in point. In public school, their

nine-year-old son Paul was earning grades far below his ability. Helen was convinced that placement in a Montessori school would make a huge difference in his life. Stan, while agreeing that public school was not the answer, felt that the discipline of a Catholic school like the one he had gone to was what Paul needed. Not simply by coincidence, the school Helen favored was close to her home, the parochial school close to Stan's.

When their otherwise-working parenting plan threatened to break down over this issue, they wisely sought a mediator. The mediator, in turn, recommended that they find and agree on an educational expert who could evaluate Paul's needs and aptitudes and provide objective information about what kind of school would work best for him. They agreed on a well-recommended educational psychologist who was familiar with all the local schools. She tested Paul and helped them to understand that he was underachieving because of a particular learning disability rather than his motivation, lack of challenge, or lack of discipline at school. It turned out that neither of the schools favored by Paul's parents had a program that would meet his needs. She recommended a third alternative, which, back in mediation, Stan and Helen were able to agree upon—and where Paul did get the help he needed.

The issue of school placement often serves as a token or symbol for a very different parental concern or motivation. Parents often use school placement to gain the validation of being the custodial parent, to punish each other, or to prove the greater strength of their concern. Paul's parents were able to put their own preferences aside once they had some accurate and unbiased information. Other parents may have continued to fight, in which case some other need may have been causing the battle. Mediation, with its focus on clarifying such underlying needs, may be very helpful in those cases.

Discipline

No two parents structure their children's lives or apply discipline identically. In fact, no parent is completely consistent in setting and enforcing the rules and patterns that shape family life. Do you treat your child just the same whether you are feeling good or bad, calm or harried, relaxed or rushed?

Nonetheless, divorcing parents are frequently concerned by the differences in lifestyle and discipline between the two homes. Mother may be strict and highly organized—these traits may well have been part of what drove Father away. On his own, he settles into an easygoing lifestyle for the children—bedtimes when tired, meals when hungry, clothes not necessarily the cleanest, baths not always taken. In addition to her concerns about the long-range effects of this lack of structure on the children, she may well have immediate problems to deal with—children coming back to her exhausted and dirty, homework not done, full from sugary treats and uninterested in her nutritious meals. "Daddy lets us," or "You're meaner than Daddy," may be hurled at her again and again. Or, the situation may be reversed—one parent may feel, with good reason, that the children are being overly inhibited, squelched, or even psychologically abused by an overly strict, too highly structured parent.

If these differences threaten to block or upset a parenting agreement, they demand solution. Several steps may be helpful.

First, both parents need to communicate accurately what their goals and approaches as parents really are. Good communication—honest talking and nondefensive listening—may reveal that their differences are less than they felt at first.

Second, the children's actual behavior in both homes needs to be watched with care. No two children have identical needs for structure, discipline, and consistency from home to home and time to time. One child may thrive on differences, gaining a wide perspective from two different lifestyles and behaving acceptably in both. Her brother or sister may become confused, angry, or manipulative in response to the same two homes.

Third, if major differences continue and one or both parents remain convinced that the children are being harmed, a hard choice needs to be made between two negatives: allowing a less-than-desirable situation to continue, or increasing parent-parent conflict by pressing the issue. No formula for making this decision exists, although I constantly remind parents that most children can tolerate differences between their homes much more readily than hostilities between their parents.

Finally, if something must be done, then applying the win-win conflict-management techniques of chapters 5, 6, and 8 becomes necessary: focus on the problem, not the people; search for underlying needs that are shared; generate a variety of potential solutions; and negotiate in a principled rather than a power-driven way.

The Bicycle on the Roof

Kirk, an active eleven-year-old, was devastated. His father had become so enraged when Kirk left his bicycle at his mother's house (for perhaps the twentieth time) that he retrieved the bicycle and threw it on the roof of his house. He told Kirk he could have it back when Kirk could prove to him that he would never leave it at his mother's house again.

Far too many divorced parents fight over clothes, toys, and other possessions. Bicycles and dolls, teddy bears and favorite clothes, homework and mittens sometimes turn into missiles in a parental war.

I asked Kirk's father, "Why don't you buy a bicycle that stays at your house?"

"It's not the expense, it's the principle of the thing."

When I asked what principle was being upheld by the bicycle on the roof, Kirk's father told me that his ex-wife needed to be more responsible, that her failure to make sure that Kirk returned with his bicycle was one more sign of her irresponsibility, more proof that she really did not care about their child.

In most cases, these fights are totally unnecessary and unjustified. Feuding parents often claim that they cannot afford to buy a second bicycle or extra clothes for the children, while at the same time they think nothing of running up enormous legal fees, "for the principle of the thing." Two working households require two refrigerators, two cars, two toaster ovens. Why not two bicycles and a happy child rather than one bicycle on the roof and a child in tears?

The commonsense principle behind successful post-divorce parenting is the creation of two good homes. This situation works best when each parent has the right to run his or her home autonomously. Most children adjust readily to different expectations and rules in different areas of their lives—for example, at home, at school, in team sports, at church. In the same way they can handle, and often benefit from, two different lifestyles and sets of rules in their parents' homes.

The Ten Keys Revisited

The same principles and approaches that helped resolve the intense feelings and conflicts during and after separation can keep things moving forward during the rebuilding period.

I. Take responsibility for your own well-being.

For many parents the rebuilding phase is a time for exploring, for opening new doors. For the first time in years a parent can make independent choices about new relationships, new career options, a new lifestyle. At the same time, this period can also be a time of severe challenges and problems. Finances may be tight or unpredictable. Schedules may be crowded by the competing demands of being a single parent, a student, and a wage earner, at the expense of time for oneself. Legal issues may still be unresolved. Mourning for the past may still not be complete, while current disagreements and hostilities may flare up unexpectedly and with devastating intensity.

During this period, the absence of a partner may be useful. For once there may be nobody else to blame for our own shortcomings. This period of self-sufficiency can be a great learning experience, teaching us that we can make it on our own, and showing us how much our happiness or unhappiness stems from what we ourselves do or fail to do. Anthropologist Paul Bohannan points out that "the psychic divorce," the task of regaining autonomy as an individual, is as important as the more obvious legal, economic, and parental aspects of divorce.

This is a time to take responsibility for creating a new home and a new life that is nurturing to you and to your children. This is a time to take responsibility for implementing, evaluating, and, when needed, modifying the agreements made earlier in your separation.

2. Be persistent—rebuilding takes time.

Completing your emotional separation, finalizing negotiations and legal agreements, putting together a new home and lifestyle, taking care of yourself and your children despite a host of challenges and changes, and doing it largely on your own can be overwhelming. Giving up can be very tempting—dropping out of school, not trying for that new job, letting the old feelings of helplessness return, sinking back into depression or futile resentment. In your dealings with your ex-spouse, giving up might mean letting the agreements you worked hard to win slip away, letting the friendly or businesslike relationship that you built deteriorate or fall apart over the differences that are bound to arise.

This loss of determination happens to many parents. In Dr. Ahrons' study, for example, 28 percent of the parents were on very friendly terms one year after their divorce. However, that percentage dropped to 9 percent over the next four years. The coparenting relationship was particularly at risk when one or both parents remarried.

Perhaps the best antidote to this risk is to be forewarned. The relief you feel when the acute trauma of separation begins to fade may lull you into a false sense of security. The trek is not yet over. Parents need to continue to use and apply all their skills to keep a good solution working, to change it judiciously when needed.

3. Create a colleague, not an enemy.

It is not easy to draw a clear boundary between your personal business and what needs to be talked over or worked out with your ex-spouse. While autonomy is vitally important, it cannot be absolute in a shared parenting situation. What you do in many areas of your life does affect the children, and hence is of legitimate concern to your ex-spouse.

Co-parenting requires reasonably open communication. It makes a lot more sense for your ex-spouse to hear about your new partner from you, early on, than from your children or a friend. I am not suggesting that you live your new life within the boundaries that your ex-spouse might prefer—clearly you do not need his or her approval for your personal decisions. But I am suggesting that you let your ex-spouse know in advance about important changes once you feel sure of them, thus reducing the risk of surprise and tempering angry reactions.

The rebuilding period is a time for strengthening the cooperative, businesslike relationship that appears to work best for most parents after divorce. It can be very helpful to view that relationship as a business partnership whose primary aim is rearing healthy, well-adjusted children. As a business partner, you dislike surprises; accordingly, you keep your partner well informed. As a business partner, you count on your associate's work; in turn, you keep your own commitments religiously. As a business partner, you expect to be listened to; naturally, you listen to your partner as well.

4. Deal with your own feelings.

By now the feelings stemming from the breakup of your marriage may be less intense. Although you may experience flare-ups of regret, frustration, depression, or anger, days or weeks may pass without these disruptions, and you are increasingly free to get on with your new life. If this is the case, you are on the right track and need little more than to enjoy the good periods and to respect your need for occasional relapses. If, however, a year or more has gone by and you are still preoccupied with negative feelings, you are faced with a serious problem and owe it to yourself and your children to take action.

You may be one of the many divorced parents who, at a deep level, has not been able to accept the death of your old relationship. How well or poorly your current parenting arrangements are going is not the primary problem, but rather your preoccupation with the relationship you have with your ex-spouse, good or bad. You may be maintaining relatively positive parenting agreements but using exchanges or communication concerning the children as an excuse for contact. Or you may continue to fight over the children and other issues, substituting forced hostility for the love that is no longer possible. Whatever the cause, a year of misery is too long. If the situation stems largely from the old relationship, individual counseling or therapy may be vital to help you let go of that old world and face the new.

Some parents continue to be the victim of feelings that stem from current difficulties rather than from the past relationship. Immediate problems such as lack of money, difficulties with the children, or stressful living conditions may be taking their toll. At times even the best parenting plan can break down because of lack of resources, a child's negative response, or the consistent failure of one parent to meet his or her responsibilities.

Carolyn had this kind of problem. She had done a good job of growing past the anger, mutual blame, and the inappropriate roles that had marked her marriage. She had pushed for mediation and, with difficulty, had worked out a reasonable custody and contact plan for their child. However, her hopes to get on with her life were frustrated when it became clear that her ex-husband Tom, a severe alcoholic, was not doing an adequate job getting his own life together, much less providing a part-time home for their daughter. When Carolyn found out that Tom had lost his job and apartment and was living in a tiny trailer on a friend's property, she realized that the shared parenting plan they had agreed on could not work.

Although she dreaded the emotional costs of "upsetting the apple cart," she tackled this problem as she had tackled many others. To her credit, she treated Tom with respect, talking to him directly about her concerns, listening to him, again asking him to mediate with her, but refusing to accept assurances and promises that experience had shown he could not keep. The results were positive. Their daughter still got to see Tom, but under conditions that guaranteed he would be sober and she would be cared for. Tom gained rather than lost self-respect through their negotiations and began improving. Carolyn, once again, was able to move forward on her own.

5. Deal with your ex's feelings.

The rebuilding period is a time for building mutual respect and understanding. A vital tool for this process is your willingness to listen to your ex-spouse. Divorced parents often seem to think that if they listen to each other, they will fall back into the trap of being controlled by the other. Listening—the kind of listening that conveys respect and increases understanding—does not have to mean either giving in to demands or digging in and resisting them.

"Michael has been coming back from your house wet and dirty."

You could respond to this kind of statement by giving in: "I'm sorry, I'll make sure he's taken a bath and wearing clean clothes no matter what." If you give in on this and other criticisms and demands, you could easily end up feeling controlled and resentful.

You could respond by resisting: "I don't tell you how to run your house, so don't tell me how to run mine." If you do, the problem will not get solved; you may have underlined your independence, but not in a way that supports future cooperation.

Or, you could respond with active listening: "You're upset because I sent Michael to you without a bath and with wet diapers."

"I sure am—you know how sensitive his skin is. I'm tired of seeing him with that rash."

"You think that if he was changed and washed more often we could get rid of his rash."

"Yes, of course."

"Fine. I'd like his rash to clear up too. Why don't we both make a concerted effort for a few weeks and see what happens?"

This parent actually combined three useful techniques for dealing with someone else's feelings—demonstrating real listening by checking what he was hearing, refusing to be provoked, and pushing for a cooperative conclusion.

6. Manage conflict through communication.

You can expect that conflicts will come up during the rebuilding phase, although one hopes not as frequently or with such intense feelings as before. However disheartening renewed troubles may be to you, this is a time to sharpen rather than set aside your conflict-management skills.

To the extent that you want to be in charge of your own home and lifestyle, you need to respect the boundaries of your child's other home as well. This respect means that you will choose to do nothing in response to many issues that may come up; you will not comment or criticize even though you do not approve. However, more serious patterns may emerge—situations that you feel, on reflection, threaten the well-being of your children and require action.

Tim faced this kind of problem some months after his ex-wife Sandra moved to a rural home. Dominic, his nine-year-old, and Leona, his five-year-old, were spending much of the summer with her. She worked, so the children were in the care of neighbors much of the time. Things seemed to go well at first, but then the children began to complain to Tim about Larry, one of the neighbors. At first the complaints did not sound serious. Tim adopted the approach of listening to the children without reacting, telling the children that the people their mother picked to take care of them were to be minded.

However, more serious questions soon arose. Both children began to return from their stays in bad moods—sometimes sullen and angry, at other times wound up and overactive. Dominic, the older child, began to complain that Larry "was weird" and "did weird things." The children answered his questions evasively, but Tim was now concerned enough to talk to Sandra. He resisted the temptation to blame her for whatever was happening, instead presenting the issue as a mutual problem. She said that the babysitting neighbors had a good reputation, but agreed to "look into it."

The pieces finally fell into place when Dominic came home with bruises on both arms. After considerable questioning, he finally told Tim that he had found and accidentally broken a bottle of liquor hidden in the garage. When Larry found out about it, he scolded him violently and told him never to tell anyone about the bottle. Leona told essentially the same story. Tim was furious that his son had been mistreated by Larry, and was deeply concerned that Larry might be abusing alcohol while responsible for the children. His impulse was to confront

Larry, to blast Sandra for her negligence, to deny her further contact with the children. To his credit, he thought things over carefully before taking any steps.

First, he called for a meeting with Sandra. There he described very factually what the children had told him. Without any threats or demands, he asked for Sandra's view of what had happened and what to do about it. Initially, Sandra was defensive. She resented Tim's intrusion into her choice of childcare, and she was not happy with the implication that she might not have checked out the daycare situation adequately. Tim responded to her defensiveness without anger. Instead he continued to present the situation as a mutual problem: both of them needed to be sure that the children were being cared for adequately. Sandra agreed with this presentation of the issue, although she insisted that the children were in good hands.

Tim persistently made three points: something had happened between Larry and the children that should not have taken place, he and she had to be concerned, and they needed to find a way to handle the problem. He offered to go with her to talk to Larry about what had happened. Sandra agreed that someone needed to talk to him but insisted that she wanted to do this on her own. Tim agreed, but insisted that the matter be cleared up before the children's next stay, unless Sandra arranged alternative daycare.

Sandra did confront Larry, and found his answers unsatisfactory. On her own initiative, she evaluated several other day-care settings and talked over the best options with Tim before choosing one. Tim's self-control, his avoidance of a personal attack on Sandra, and his focus on a joint attack on the problem allowed them to solve a potentially explosive matter.

7. Manage conflict through action.

When a marriage starts to break down and during the chaotic time around separation, boundaries become unclear. One or both partners may try to act completely independently, taking unilateral steps that ignore the other partner's needs and interests. At the same time, separating parents may try to enforce inappropriate or impossible levels of control—for example, trying to prevent the other from dating, or continuing to "drop in" as if both parents still lived in the same house. Unclear boundaries lead to confusion, hurt, and anger. Much of the fighting that takes place following separation has the unconscious aim of drawing new boundaries within the family.

When the battles are fought successfully, the result is a new kind of family structure. Once again, boundaries are clear. Each parent has won a large area of independence and is free to build a new life without having to deal with the wishes of the other. At the same time, they continue to be interdependent in one crucial area: they continue to share communication and decision making where the children are concerned. The key to success during the rebuilding period is to expand and enjoy your areas of independence, while clearly recognizing and respecting that much-reduced part of your life—the children—where you remain interdependent with your ex-partner, and where a continuing businesslike relationship is needed.

8. Find out what you and your ex *really* want.

In any conflict or potential conflict with your ex-spouse, you must avoid clinging to prechosen positions—"The children *must* spend Christmas with their grandparents!"—and instead search together for more basic needs.

"But they've always been with my parents at Christmas."

"I know, but that's when we were together. Now, the children have two homes. I want them to know what Christmas is like at my home too."

"My parents will be terribly hurt, and the children will be so disappointed if they don't go."

"To me Christmas means more than just a lot of presents and making grandparents happy. It means sharing something as a family, it means giving to each other, it's supposed to be a happy time, not an obligation."

"Of course, I feel that way too. What are you suggesting?"

Once these two parents can agree on what they hope the children will experience at Christmas, they can explore a variety of possibilities. If they defend surface positions, Christmas, or any other issue, will become one more power struggle.

It sometimes helps during the rebuilding phase to get away—

even if that can only be for a few hours, a day, or a weekend. With that extra perspective it becomes possible to look beyond your immediate needs and troubles, to catch a glimpse of your larger goals. How do you want your life to be going six months, one year, five years from today? How do you want your children's lives to be structured at those times? How do you see your children in that not-so-distant future?

9. Explore options: In search of the win-win-win solution.

The rebuilding period is a time for exploration. Both in your dealings with your ex-spouse and in the independent areas of your life, this is a time to break out of limiting old habits, to open new doors for yourself and your children. It is exciting, sometimes frightening, to have more freedom. Unless you are one of those rare people who knows exactly what your goals are, the best way to find out is by exploring, by trying out new approaches in many areas of your life.

You may know people who have grasped the chance that a divorce gave them to make significant changes in their lives. It is commonplace these days to see divorced parents going back to school, launching new careers, making new friends, taking up new activities, trying out different ways of parenting, and forming new and often better relationships.

Parenting is one area where changes can be especially fruitful. Current research shows that, depending on their age and maturity, many children thrive on the greater stimulation and socialization they get in well-run day care than in the more sheltered home environment. Although children should not be burdened by becoming a parent's confidant or counselor, many children are more than ready to cope with a larger share of the work and responsibilities of a home headed by a single parent. Many of the brightest and best-functioning teenagers I have met have come from homes where the discipline and hard work of a parent inspired the children's respect and acceptance of responsibility.

10. Negotiate.

For most people, the hardest negotiations will have taken place earlier, ideally leading to a parenting agreement providing security and stability for the rebuilding period. However, unforeseen events can easily provoke new controversy at times requiring renewed confrontation and negotiation.

Remarriage is one of the biggest sources of change and conflict for divorced parents. Everyone must adapt—the new mate, the children, the previous partner, and the parent who is remarrying. New boundaries need to be drawn between the two households, and this redefinition is often very hard to do. Chapter 11 deals with this area in detail.

A second area that often leads to serious differences is a proposed move. Many parents, for personal, financial, or career reasons, need or want to move, sometimes thousands of miles away. Clearly any major move will force changes in whatever parenting plan has been in operation. In addition, a move may reduce the available options. No longer can parents choose from among many different schedules providing the children with adequate time in each home. A problem of this magnitude has no simple solution. However, the way parents choose to reach a solution can make all the difference in the world.

Many children, too many, develop serious emotional problems in the aftermath of a parent's impulsive, one-sided move. The worst off are children who have been stolen by one parent away from another. Frightened, confused, distrustful, often abused, many require years of treatment. Children who feel abandoned are also common. When there has been inadequate preparation, when continuing contact with both parents has not been provided for, children experience the disappearance of a parent from their lives. They are left feeling bereft and powerless. Children who have been dragged by an unstable parent from place to place, or who have been sent from home to home because of their parents' inability to create a stable parenting plan, may also be badly hurt.

A planned move is important enough to require careful thought, communication with one's ex-spouse and children, and whatever amount of mutual problem solving is needed to come to a realistic and livable solution for all concerned. As in any negotiation, four concepts can guide you:

1. Separate the people from the problem. Once it is clear that a move needs to be made, it is vital to focus on the problem rather than the people.

"My finances are making this move necessary," not "If you supported us like you should, I wouldn't have to move."

"I recognize your need to be closer to your family," not "You'll never stop being Momma's Boy, will you?"

"I need to have the kids here as much as possible," not "You're just trying to destroy my relationship with the kids, just like you always have."

2. Focus on interests, not positions. If you can identify your own and your ex-spouse's real needs, a positive solution becomes much more likely. Perhaps the real need is not for a better job, but for more independence. Can that need be met in another way? Perhaps the real need is not to be closer to family, but to have enough time away from the children to meet one's personal needs. How can that happen without a move? Perhaps the real need is to hurt the other spouse. Frank recognition of such an underlying motive may reduce some of the pressure to act.

3. Generate options. Flexibility is crucial in this kind of situation. Perhaps the move can be postponed. Perhaps both parents can move to the same geographic area. Perhaps both parents can agree that the children will benefit from the move or from an extended period of time with one parent. Perhaps the school year and the summer will provide a natural framework for a workable schedule. Perhaps a school can be found that divides the year into four equal periods. Perhaps the younger children will do better in one area or with one parent, the older with the other. If enough options can be found, one is likely to emerge with a plan that best meets the underlying needs of both parents and children—the "win-win-win" solution.

4. Insist on an objective standard. It may well be helpful to seek external advice. An educational psychologist might be able to offer important information about the kind of school placement a child needs. A child therapist may be able to advise about your child's probable response to different custodial

plans. A full-scale evaluation of the children and parents may show that one or another of the possible options is much better for the children. Particularly if the proposed move is being made to meet one parent's needs, and is opposed because it threatens the needs of the other parent, agreeing to use the children's best interests as an objective standard can be of great help.

Rebuilding—getting on with your life in the aftermath of a divorce—hinges on one crucial concept: you and your ex-spouse must define that area in which your children's needs force you to remain interdependent and work out an adequate way of relating within that area. Your ability to create and maintain businesslike or friendly communication about your children will make the difference between freedom and failure. If you and your ex-spouse can draw the boundaries of that area with bold, clear strokes and can find the strength to overcome your anger and animosities in order to deal with each other effectively, then both of you will be free to explore and build new, independent lives.

CHAPTER 11

Remarriage:
Coping with Change

Individuals and families change constantly, and rarely more rapidly than in the years following divorce. Change can threaten or upset the arrangements and agreements parents have painfully worked out, forcing them, however reluctantly, to pour their energy into dealing with family problems once again.

Researchers, therapists, and parents agree that the most difficult challenges are encountered when a parent remarries. The great hopes and expectations that the new couple shares often crash against the realities and complexities of forming a new family unit in the aftermath of divorce. Parents and children experience painful loyalty conflicts. A host of new relationships must be worked out, both within the new family and between that unit and the new partners' ex-spouses. New roles have to be created, roles that our society still has not understood or approved, as indicated by the negative associations the words "stepparent" and "stepchild" carry. We have few models for these complex new families.

The problems and prejudices blended families face are certainly not due to their scarcity. Currently about 80 percent of divorced men and 70 percent of divorced women remarry within three years of divorce. The result—nearly ten thousand blended families are formed each week in the United States and Canada. Today more than one-third of the children in North America live in families in which at least one parent is remarried. Statisticians predict that before long, remarried couples will head more families than first-marriage couples.

If you are already part of a "yours, mine, and ours" family, you are probably aware of the kinds and the intensity of problems blended families face. If you are not yet in this situation, even if you expect difficulties, you may be surprised by how hard the reality can be. Perhaps you can benefit from the experience of parents who have preceded you.

The Reconstituted Family: Just Add Love and Stir?

"The first thing I realized," Susan confided, "was that this was never going to be like I'd dreamed—a simple, close, loving family, kind of like I had growing up, or even in my first marriage."

"That's for sure," added Jim, her second husband. "Neither of us had any idea what it would really be like."

Susan and Jim, like most remarrying parents, had only one model for the new family they hoped to form—the traditional family of father, mother, and their children. Consciously or unconsciously, they expected their marriage to create an instant family. They imagined themselves and the children coming together to regain the same sense of security, the same feeling of belonging, the same shared love, the same easy give and take of a nuclear family.

They, like many parents, were victims of a myth. The traditional nuclear family and the new blended family differ in basic ways. Perhaps these differences will be clearer if we compare a nuclear family with a blended one.

Nuclear Family	Blended Family
Two (young) adults fall in love, forming one couple.	Four divorced parents who have lost in love form one couple plus two "outside" parents.
After some time to grow as a couple, together they produce one or more babies.	From the moment they meet, children are already present.
Biology ensures that they and their children are bonded, love each other.	Biology divides them into "yours, mine, and ours."

| Each child gains two loving parents. | Each child loses a special relationship with a parent. |

Although there may be rivalries and conflicts within the family, there is unquestioned loyalty to it.

There are powerful rivalries within the new family, *and* conflicted loyalty to a second family.

Society accepts, values, and protects this kind of family.

Society does not yet fully accept, value, or protect this family.

Many parents and children do come to live happily in blended families. However, they achieve this level of acceptance through hard work and by understanding and respecting personal differences and family complexity, not by trying to become what they are not—a nuclear family.

Needed: New Rules, New Roles, New Rituals

"Jim and I were so happy to have found each other that it never occurred to us that the children wouldn't feel the same way," said Susan.

"Actually," Jim corrected, "the children fooled us to some extent. My kids, especially Beth [his five-year-old], liked Susan a lot while we were dating. Stuart [her eleven-year-old] and I got along pretty well until we all moved in together."

"Yes," Susan laughed, "and then things really fell apart. His kids, especially Robert—a big, strong twelve-year-old— wouldn't listen to me at all. Stuart walked around hating the world, and especially Jim. He and Robert fought constantly— they couldn't be in the same room together. I was yelling at Stuart all the time, but I got furious if Jim tried to discipline him. Beth wouldn't eat anything I cooked. It took us six months just to get through a meal without a fight."

One of the first tasks a blended family faces is agreeing on the basics—cooking and mealtimes, who sleeps where, who does what jobs, who has the right to tell someone else what to do, how to handle disagreements. Susan and Jim had not dealt with these issues before they got together, so they ran headlong into them when they moved into their new house.

Susan was used to running a fairly disciplined household, one with clear rules where children did pretty much as they were told. That was how she had been raised, and she had found that this worked well with Stuart after her divorce. She believed that her firmness was the only reason she had not run into the same kind of trouble with him that some single mothers had with their boys.

Not until Jim and Susan were living together did they realize that their views of childrearing were totally different. Jim still carried angry feelings at his own parents because of their over-control and harsh discipline; he wanted his children to be much more independent than he had been. He encouraged them to question even his own authority and prided himself on always being willing to talk with them. When Susan issued an order, she expected it to be obeyed without question. Robert and Beth rebelled. Jim sided with his children on this issue; in fact he often got angrier at Susan than either of the children did. It did not take long before Susan realized that unless significant changes were made, she would soon be cast permanently in the role of wicked stepmother.

Practical Matters

How many of these basic areas of family life have you and your new spouse worked out together?

1. Where will the new family live?
2. Where will the money come from? Will it be enough? Will it be reliable?
3. How will financial matters be handled? By whom?
4. How will available space be divided? Where will everyone sleep? Who will be losing space? Who will be intruding on someone else's territory?
5. What is each parent's philosophy about discipline?
6. Who will discipline which children?

7. How will differences concerning discipline be resolved?

8. Who will be doing the cooking? Cleaning up? Shopping?

9. Are you going to have family meals? Snacks between meals?

10. What kind of food is acceptable?

11. How are children expected to behave while eating?

12. How are other household chores and responsibilities going to be divided?

13. What are your attitudes about sexuality? Walking around dressed or half-dressed? Bathing or sleeping together?

14. What about alcohol and drug use? What is acceptable? By whom?

15. How seriously do you take obligations such as paying bills, arriving on time, making and keeping promises?

16. What will the children call the two of you? What last names will each family member use?

17. Is it acceptable to express disagreement? Anger? Aggression? If so, in what ways?

18. What kind and amount of relationship will the children be encouraged to maintain with their other parent?

19. What kind and amount of relationship will each of you maintain with your ex-spouses?

20. What about grandparents? Holidays? Gifts?

Young adults marrying for the first time usually have time together to reach agreements about these issues. Many blended families find themselves thrown together with conflicting, sometimes incompatible ideas and habits in these areas. Blended families are happier when they work these issues out, or at least talk seriously about them, before moving in together.

Who's in Charge Here?

"I really thought I would go crazy," Susan continued. "I kept expecting us to kind of melt together and get to be one family. But what happened is that we split right down the middle—Jim, Robert, and Beth lined up against Stuart and me. I really believed that I would love Jim's children just like I love Stuart. Instead I found out I didn't even *like* them. It's hard to admit, but sometimes I really hated them because they were acting like the worst kind of spoiled brats and they were driving Jim and me apart."

Jim nodded his agreement. "There were several times when we came awfully close to separating because of the kids. The only thing that held us together was how we felt about each other, how we got along together the few times we were alone. Neither of us was willing to give that up."

The pressures and stresses of blended families are so strong that they fail three times as frequently as first marriages and twice as frequently as remarriages without stepchildren. The only glue powerful enough to make them work is love. Not the hoped-for love between stepparents and stepchildren—that love may take years to develop if it ever does. Not love between stepsiblings—their rivalries may go on for years. Only when two parents love each other deeply, passionately, and with great commitment are they likely to bridge the gaps that divide them and their children and go on to build a real family.

In addition, that couple has to put its love into action. Family therapists use the term "executive couple" to describe parents who work together effectively to accomplish the difficult job of raising children. Like the leadership of a corporation, parents must set the tone and wield ultimate authority in the new family. They need to sort out their differences quickly and efficiently, so that they can give a clear, unified message to the children.

Any family will have problems if one parent monopolizes responsibility, if one parent gives up meaningful parenting, or if parents cannot agree on how to deal with the children. However, living in a blended family is like being connected to a powerful amplifier. What would have been a minor argument in a nuclear family can easily become an ear-shattering battle. What might have been a door-slamming fight in a nuclear family may threaten to blow a blended family apart.

It took a major crisis to force Jim and Susan to start to work together as an executive couple.

"I guess," Jim reported, shaking his head, "Stuart decided he just couldn't take it any more."

"He'd always been an only child," Susan explained, "so he never had to share or compete with other children. Then, after my divorce, I relied on him a lot—he and I became very close. Sometimes I'd hear him bragging to his friends about being the man in the house."

"We didn't think about it until later," Jim continued, "but when we got married, Stuart lost a lot that mattered to him. He'd already lost the family he'd grown up in. To a large extent he lost a very close relationship with his father. Then Susan and I got together and he lost his special relationship with her, and finally he lost his privileges as an only child."

"It all came out," Susan said quietly, "when he lured Robert out to the backyard to show him something, and then hit him over the head with a pipe. He could have killed him."

Jim looked at her for a long time. "That's when we realized how out-of-control we were. We started to talk, really talk about how we felt, and we got into family therapy."

Although not every blended family goes through an experience as traumatic as theirs, most do experience the kind of strains that led up to it. Stepparents come to recognize that love between themselves and their stepchildren, or between the children themselves, is not going to be instant. Children, particularly children of divorce, often resent and resist the new family unit. This attitude is not surprising. A parent's remarriage strikes a fatal blow to their fantasies of their parents getting back together again. Any remaining anger that they feel is likely to surface. Rather than give up this protective fantasy, children may work to break up the new marriage. Children, like adults, need time to mourn for the loss of their family. An early remarriage may bring a child's unresolved grief to the surface. Even when a parent is ready to be vulnerable and love again, a child may not.

To a parent, divorce may mean freedom from an unhappy or intolerable situation and allow longed-for independence. Children lose the only security and happiness they have known, frequently lose adequate access to one parent, and are tossed helplessly on the roller coaster of their parents' feelings.

When a parent remarries, he or she gains a new mate and partner, new financial and emotional security, and the status of marriage. Children lose the extra-close relationship with their primary parent that often develops after divorce, and also may lose their prized position as an only child, the youngest child, the oldest boy or girl, etc.

Their reactions are all too familiar. Some children become depressed, angry, sullen, or hostile. Some throw a tantrum at the wedding ceremony; others start talking baby talk again or stop talking entirely. Some begin to wet or soil themselves. Some refuse to mind or shift into slow motion every time they are asked to do something. Some children hate each other or hate their stepparents. Teenagers sometimes fail in school, run away, become delinquent or sexually promiscuous. Children, in short, will sometimes do everything they can to split this threatening new family down the seams, to get back to the way things were.

"The counseling made me realize that I didn't have to feel guilty because I didn't love Jim's children, or blame them for not loving me. What our counselor said really made sense—the first thing to do was to protect ourselves and earn the children's respect. Later we might find friendship or even love."

"I never expected," Jim responded, "to feel the same way about Stuart as I did about my own kids, so I didn't have the same kind of guilt as Susan. But I also didn't expect Stuart to be able to get to me the way he did. I'd take one look at that sullen face and be angry the rest of the day."

"For me it got to be sink or swim. I loved Susan, and if I wanted to stay with her, we had to make the family work. After the pipe incident there just wasn't any room for disagreement about how to handle the kids."

When parents accept the myth of instant love toward their stepchildren, they almost always find instant guilt instead. Love, as Susan learned, may develop eventually, but it has to be based on respect and friendship and grow over time. The new family is not like a blanket bought neat and clean at the store; it is more like a patchwork quilt, pieced together from many different sources, the seams stitched with patience and care. This painstaking job, if it is going to work, needs to be done together. If one parent unravels what the other has done, the children's agitation will soon tear the developing family apart.

"Some friends of ours taught us a big lesson," Susan smiled slightly, "although they didn't realize it. We went to dinner at their house, and we could see that they were making the same mistakes we were, only worse. Dee was trying so hard to stay in control of her husband's kids that she was giving orders like an army sergeant."

"Worse," Jim broke in, "at least a sergeant lets people eat."

"She had so many rules," Susan went on, "that nobody could eat. One of her rules was that the children had to keep their hands above the table all the time. Just enforcing that kept her and everyone else on edge constantly. I wasn't at all surprised when dinner turned into a fiasco. I could see myself in her, and I decided I would never let things get that bad with us."

"And what I saw," Jim added, "was that Dave had pulled out entirely. He had handed over discipline of his children to Dee, which was impossible at that point in time, and he wasn't being honest with her about how he felt. In fact, they split up a few months later."

Each parent faces a delicate balancing task. To come on too strong, demanding more love or more obedience than the children can give, is a recipe for disaster. To pull back too far, refusing to engage with a child, failing to take care of one's own needs, leaves a gaping hole in the fabric of the family.

This task changes with time. Most stepparents find that a low-key approach works best at first. They should be clear about their own needs—no one is helped by allowing a child to make life miserable—and they must support each other, do enough talking and win-win negotiating to bring about that mutual support. They need to make and maintain meaningful contact with the children. However, it almost always works better to let the children's feelings for a stepparent grow rather than forcing them.

Later, when stepparents and stepchildren share a history of respect, care, and friendship, the relationship will be able to bear more weight. Beth may start to call Susan "Mom." Stuart may talk to Jim about a problem rather than sulking or calling his father. Arguments will flare up less intensely and be forgotten more quickly. Direction and discipline, when given, can be accepted. Schoolwork and chores are accepted with less protest.

Nonetheless, creating a successfully blended family takes a lot of time. Although young children, especially preschoolers, often accept a new parent figure readily, older children and teenagers need much more time to develop trust, respect, and affection. Most parents go through three, four, or even five years of turmoil and hard work before their new family really starts to feel like and work as a unit.

It is useful, especially with older children and teenagers, to be clear that you *do not* expect them to love you. This permission to have their own feelings frees them from obligation and guilt, clearing the way for a real relationship to develop.

Yours, Mine, Ours, and Theirs

"The next big problem," Jim explained, "was between Susan and my ex-wife. I had worked out a pretty good system with my ex. Each of us had the kids half time. We lived a few blocks from each other, so moving the kids back and forth once a week wasn't hard, and it didn't disrupt their school or friendships. Several of my friends had gone through horrible custody fights, so I knew what a good thing we had going."

"What happened," Susan said, "was that I resented the time Jim spent on the phone with her, and when I would see them chatting away so comfortably when she picked up the kids, I'd get furious. Jim and I were having a lot of troubles, and Robert and Beth were driving me up the wall. Seeing her getting along so well with Jim and the children made me feel incredibly insecure."

Conflicts involving the "other parent" come in many forms. In their drive to recreate a nuclear family, remarried parents are tempted to exclude the other parent. Even when such exclusion does not happen, the remarriage of an ex-spouse can be extremely threatening to a parent—some degree of jealousy is almost universal. A parent may feel that his or her relationship to the children is in danger, that the new wife or husband will somehow woo the children away. Second wives often try too hard, either to win the children's affection through affection and indulgence, or to prove themselves by being supercapable, supercaring, or superfirm. Second husbands can easily come to see their wives' cooperation with ex-husbands as exploitation. Many encourage their wives to take a harder line, or themselves jump directly into the fray as a champion. This intrusive involvement can easily lead to hostilities, even after years of relative calm. New spouses often feel insecure or jealous over any contact between their new mate and his or her ex. They may pressure their partners to cut off even necessary communication, reduce support, or join them in criticizing or insulting their perceived rivals.

"Susan's hostility towards my ex-wife put me right in the middle," Jim remarked, looking at Susan. "I had no desire to do anything more with her than I had to so that the joint custody would work. But Susan reacted like I was having an affair."

"Luckily," Susan replied, "our counselor helped on that too. She told us that the *better* kids relate to one parent, the *easier* it is for them to accept a stepparent. It's the kids who are on really shaky ground with their real mom who don't dare open up to stepmom. That really helped me to stop feeling so threatened by her. Plus I realized that Jim just wasn't going to change his way of relating to her."

If you put yourself in a child's place, this insight makes very good sense. Suppose your relationship with your father is very shaky. After the divorce he moved away. You miss him terribly. There is a hole in your life where he used to be. On the rare occasions you get to see him, your hopes are shattered—he spends most of his time arguing with your mother instead of loving you. Are you going to feel free to accept whatever your mother's new husband has to offer you, or are you going to push him away out of fear that caring for him will push your real father even farther away? Having been hurt so deeply by your real father, are you going to be able to open up, and so become vulnerable, to another? Research clearly bears out this phenomenon. Children with a secure relationship to *both* divorced parents accept a stepparent and adapt much more readily to a parent's remarriage than children with insecure, distant, or hostile relationships to one or both parents.

"One thing that made living with Stuart even harder," Jim went on, "was his feelings about his father. His father is kind of a grown-up hippie. Right now we think he might be in Boston, but Stuart might get a call from him next week from somewhere in Oregon."

"Or," Susan tossed in, "Stuart might not hear from him for six months. Then he'll call from the airport and want to drop by in an hour."

"What this does," Jim explained, "is make Stuart totally preoccupied with this mysterious father. If he doesn't hear from him he gets depressed. If he does hear, it's at the wrong time, or not enough, so he is disappointed or hurt. If I pat him on the back, he's thinking, 'That doesn't count 'cause you're not my dad.' If I scold him, he's thinking, 'If Dad were here, I wouldn't have to take this.'"

"Our counselor described it like a lens," Susan said. "Everything a child experiences is filtered through his feelings about his parents. Stuart's feelings about his father are so mixed up that he can't even begin to see Jim as he really is."

"Part of the reason that we've had a slightly easier time with Robert and Beth," Jim contrasted, "is that they've got a much better relationship with their mother and with me. They didn't have to feel like traitors if they were friendly toward Susan. They still don't love her like they do their mom, but they are starting to like her."

A child's loyalty to a parent is one of the most powerful forces we encounter. In the storm of divorce, a child may cling desperately to a present or absent parent, pushing away anyone else who tries to fill that role. Stepparents need to realize and be clear that they are not trying to replace Mom or Dad—parents just are not replaceable. In most families, a stepparent will do much better by helping to quiet the emotional storms than by making a direct attempt to win a child's affections or fill the role of disciplinarian.

Jim is now trying to apply what he learned in counseling. He tries to speak positively to Stuart about his father. He is starting to see Stuart's sullenness and anger as depression instead of hostility, and to respond by talking empathically to Stuart about his feelings rather than by being provoked into a fight.

"Two weeks ago Stuart had his birthday. We had a party, but it was ruined for Stuart because nothing came from his father. Yesterday he got a card from his father, but he wouldn't read it. A year ago all I would have seen was his long face and his anger, and I would have jumped on him. When he threw the card away, I picked it up and told him, 'I'm going to save this just in case you feel more like reading it later.' Today he asked me for it— and he didn't flinch when I gave him a hug."

It may not seem like a lot, but this small, respectful exchange is a world away from the battles Stuart and Jim were having a year ago. It represents one neatly tied stitch pulling the seams of this still-new family closer together.

Jim and Susan have progressed along a difficult path shared by thousands of other blended families. Their first stage was one of hopes and dreams centering around recreating a nuclear family to replace what they and their children had lost. As so many blended families discover, these fantasies are very different from reality. Susan and Jim hoped to make their children happy but instead found increased conflict and anger. They expected to love their stepchildren and be loved in return but were ignored and rejected—the children's hopes and dreams did not include them. They hoped as a couple to share the burdens of parenting, but instead found their differences about parenting pulling them apart.

Suggestions for Parents in Blended Families

1. Remarry for the right reasons. A great deal of love and commitment are needed to make a blended family work. If your goals are primarily to improve your finances, be less lonely, gain security, or "help" your children, there are easier and better ways to reach them.

2. Give yourself plenty of time. It takes most people at least two years after a divorce to be ready for a serious new relationship.

3. Bring issues and differences out into the open. The forces in blended families are too strong to be handled without open communication and energetic problem solving.

4. Don't try to recreate a nuclear family; a blended family has a different history, different feelings, and different roles.

5. Make every effort to include the children's other parent in their lives. Children adjust better to remarriage when they have secure, positive relationships with both of their parents.

6. Apply win-win problem solving to the children's other parents. Work with them in a businesslike way whenever possible.

7. Expect that the children will not be as happy about their new lives as you feel (or hope to). They are at least as likely to resent and resist this change as they are to appreciate and cooperate with it.

8. Forget the myth of instant love between stepparents and stepchildren. Love, if it develops, must follow respect and friendship patiently won. With older chil-

dren, make it clear that you *do not* expect them to love you.

9. The same is true for instant love between stepsiblings. Intense rivalries may develop, especially when children are displaced from familiar and cherished roles, and between children of the same sex who are close in age.

10. Work to minimize the children's losses by respecting their space, giving them adequate time, maintaining their meaningful rights and responsibilities, and recognizing their special roles in the family.

11. It is not appropriate to ask for your child's approval for your remarriage. However, once you start to be serious about living together, include the children as much as is possible and appropriate to their ages, in shared activities, planning, and the steps towards a new life together.

12. Once you are serious about living together, be open with the children about your feelings and plans. Although children can easily be overstimulated by too-open sexuality, do not attempt to hide the fact that you have become a couple.

13. The stronger the couple, the stronger the new family. Protect and nurture yourselves as a couple. Give yourselves private time together.

14. Work together as a united "executive couple." Support each other's parenting decisions whenever possible. When you cannot support each other, work your differences out in private as quickly and meaningfully as you can.

15. Recognize that discipline is ineffective unless there is also affection and trust. Relationship building often takes two years or more. Until your relationship with a stepchild can support meaningful discipline, it may be best to hand serious issues over to your mate.

16. As your relationships with your stepchildren develop, find a balance between being withdrawn or indulgent and smothering or overcontrolling.

17. Make it clear that you are not trying to become or replace Mom or Dad—they are not replaceable.

18. Younger children, especially those under eight, accept a stepparent more readily than older children can. Rather than expecting older children to see you as a parent, respect and support their relationship with their biological parents.

19. Sibling rivalries can be devastating in blended families. Make a conscious effort to treat the children as fairly as possible. Avoid favoritism as much as possible. Insist that grandparents and other family members avoid playing favorites too—for example, by giving holiday gifts to all the children.

20. Be cautious about trying to change the children's surnames. Names have powerful symbolic value. Needless changes can easily heighten loyalty conflicts and provoke renewed battles.

Gradually Susan and Jim became more aware of the need for change. However, like many couples, they did not start to deal with family strains effectively until a crisis forced them to. At that point they had little choice but to bring their differences out into the open. Although it was by no means easy, they were able to work through their disagreements concerning parenting, start to support each other as parents, and become an effective executive couple. As they became closer, opportunities for the children to divide them diminished. The children began to realize that this family was "for real" and gradually started to make the best of it.

Although Jim and Susan benefited from counseling, many couples find solutions on their own. What seems to be common to those families who stay together past the crisis point is a strong, loving couple committed to staying together; honest, effective communication; sensitivity to feelings and family dynamics; and the willingness to give up old ideas and try new ones.

Jim and Susan have now reached a new level of intimacy, in many ways deeper than either of them experienced in their previous marriages. Although neither of them likes conflict, both of them have learned how quickly dishonesty, unaired differences, unexpressed feelings, lead to explosions in the charged atmosphere of their new family. So they are honest with each other, sometimes painfully so. The result is, as Jim describes it, "a clean relationship—we may not always be happy with each other, but we always know where we stand."

Their relationships with their stepchildren are also moving toward intimacy—not the instant love they so unrealistically expected, but hard-won acceptance, grudging respect, and the beginnings of affection.

"For a while," Susan admits, "all I was interested in was surviving. I figured if I could make it a day at a time I was doing pretty well. But now, I'm actually starting to live again and see that sometimes it can even be fun. I think for me the shift came when I started thinking about things outside the family, and especially when I took a new job."

Her renewed hopes are on much firmer ground than her old fantasies. Researchers have found that, in blended families that stay together, more than 80 percent of parents describe their relationships with their stepchildren as good or excellent. Although forming a blended family is clearly stressful for parents and children, follow-up studies of stepchildren suggest that they do benefit over time from the new family unit.

The ultimate test of a blended family, ironically, is not how long it stays together, but how well it handles the next stage of any healthy family—children growing up and leaving home, as confident, independent, well-functioning young adults.

CHAPTER 12

Growing Up Winners

I spoke to Karyn just a week before her eighteenth birthday. She radiated all the excitement and energy of a vibrant young woman impatient to get on with her life. She could only spare a few hours for our interview, she told me breathlessly, because she was rehearsing for a school play, organizing a state meeting of her youth group, and meeting with a friend to plan their visit to the string of colleges they were considering. She was dizzyingly busy and enjoying every minute of it.

When I asked about her parent's divorce, her expressive face revealed a kaleidoscope of feelings. After a long pause she explained, "My mom and dad have stayed friends, and that's been really good. Since I was little, we've always had Christmas together, and, like last night, we all had dinner together to talk about my college. Not to exaggerate, they're not like best friends, but at least they get along and we can be together and it's not all hard.

"There are even some benefits of having divorced parents," she went on. "I've always gone on more vacations than other kids and gotten two sets of presents. My parents' lifestyles are really different, so I picked up and learned different things from both of them. I've gotten such a wide variety of experiences that I probably wouldn't have had if they were together.

"I know it wasn't easy for them to keep as good relations as they have—they're so different as people. I don't think many people have divorces as good as theirs—most people aren't that strong. I've met people just like them, and I know these people are normal, but something happens to them when they get a divorce that makes them weird. I respect it a lot that my parents had the ability to deal with each other enough to make things the best they could for me.

"I'm really happy they did work it out the way they did because I have friends whose parents got divorced and they lived with their mom or their dad and saw the other one once a year. I think that's awful. I think that is the worst thing. I can't believe people do that to their kids."

In these few words Karyn voiced the key question for divorcing parents today: will they have the strength to deal with each other well enough to make things work out for their children? If they can find that strength, chances are good that they can rebuild their lives and that their children will be able to live up to their potentials. Unlike Karyn, most eighteen-year-olds will not have the perspective and self-confidence to be able to comment so clearly about their parents, but their ability to go out into the world as independent and happy young adults will be comment enough.

It was clear to Karyn that strength, the kind of strength children desperately need their parents to have, is shown not by fighting for control and dominance, but by finding ways to get along "well enough," not by winning a custody battle, but by struggling to create a winning solution for mother, father, and child.

Karyn knew that her parents' divorce was not without pain. She showed me family pictures from the time of the divorce and pointed out how unhappy all of them looked. The pictures reminded her of the mixed-up years after the separation, when her mother was struggling to start her career and her father was involved with several different women, a time when she felt hurt and resentful. "Until a few years ago," she confided, "I used to get really sad because Mom and Dad weren't together. Sometimes I'd get mad at Mom and tell her how she'd ruined my whole life."

As we talked, it became clear that she and her parents had weathered several difficult transitions. Her mother Joan had gone back to school soon after the divorce. Under their initial agreement, Karyn spent the bulk of her time with her father Don. She remembered how close she and her father grew during those years.

"My memories are like in pictures. I see a lot of pictures of me with my dad, and it seems like we were real close around that time. I think I felt, even though I was just a little girl, like I had to take care of Dad. Then my mom met another man and was living with him and then got married and I hated him, so maybe I got even closer to Dad. I still saw Mom a lot, but I was happier living with Dad."

When Karyn was twelve, her mother divorced for the second time. With her disliked stepfather out of the way, Karyn became much closer to her mother. She found that it was a lot easier to talk to her mother than to her father about "important things." She began to talk about living with her mother, which created the next family crisis.

"I'd just started junior high," she said, "and it was just too hard to keep switching clothes around. I think that's what it was . . . oh yeah, and Mom had lots more time for me then. I definitely talk easier with her, like I can tell her stuff about my feelings. She loves talking everything out and reasoning. Anyway, I told her I wanted to live with her, and she told Dad, and pretty soon I moved in with her."

To her parents' credit, Karyn is not aware of what her parents went through to accept and adjust to this development. Her father remembers it distinctly.

"Several changes happened all at once. Karyn's mother split up with Peter. That made it more conducive for Karyn to spend time there. Joan had finished school and gotten her career going by then, so she was ready to give Karyn more attention. Although it was not a crucial factor, Karyn's junior high was closer to Joan's house.

"I was very much against the change for a long time. At first I was angry—I thought that Joan was pulling on Karyn, trying to make her feel guilty about living with me. But Karyn would come home as happy as could be and babble about how terrific her mom was, how happy she was there, how much fun it was to go shopping with her, put on makeup, whatever. Meanwhile Joan was being pretty reasonable. She wasn't yelling at me or demanding an immediate change, just pointing out that Karyn's needs were changing. After a while I realized that, for whatever reasons, Karyn really needed her mother then, more than she needed to be living with me."

"It took the whole school year for us to work it out," Joan explained. "When Karyn first starting saying she wanted to live with me, I told her that I loved her and wanted to spend more time with her, but that her father and I were not going to make a quick decision. I talked to Don about it, but in a very low-key way. I expected him to be upset, since they were so close, and I was right.

"I encouraged Karyn to talk to her father about what she wanted, but she found that very hard to do. She's always been very up front about her feelings to me, sometimes too much, but for whatever reasons she's always been less sure of their relationship. She seems to need to take care of his feelings. So I would tell Don that she was still bringing it up. After a few months he admitted to me that she was making it clear to him too, one way or another, that she wanted to be with me."

"When I started to focus on what Karyn needed, instead of what I was feeling," Don admitted, "I knew that some kind of change was needed. But it felt like I would be losing her, and that hurt so much that I couldn't make the decision on my own. So around January of that year I told Joan that it would be OK with me to send Karyn to a psychologist for a few visits, to find out from a neutral person what was going on with her. I didn't promise to go along with the therapist's recommendations, but the implication was there."

They sent Karyn to a mutually agreed-upon therapist. After several visits the therapist reported back to them that Karyn was genuinely motivated to live with her mother, and that this desire was appropriate for a girl her age.

"Even after the psychologist's report," Joan recalled, "nothing happened. I guess Don just couldn't give her up without a fight. After two months and a lot of worrying, I arranged a meeting with him and the therapist to talk things over. At the meeting I finally insisted that we make a decision. I knew that Don and I had a pretty good level of cooperation, and I didn't want to spoil that. But I also knew that if I was ever going to stand up for what Karyn needed, that was the time."

"Karyn made it clear," reflected Don, "that we couldn't just keep putting off a decision. To her credit she didn't blame me or issue any ultimatums. She just said that for her sake we needed to decide soon. I think it was the therapist who recommended mediation. Anyway, I agreed to mediate, we went for one or two sessions, and we agreed to reverse the time schedule. Since then Karyn's spent most of her time at Joan's, although she calls me or drops by my office almost every day."

"The mediator was great," Joan remembered, "but it was still really hard. Don was angry, defensive, and he came up with a thousand reasons why Karyn should stay with him. Not screaming at him was one of the hardest things I've ever done. But at a certain point the mediator pointed out how anguished Don was. I remember him using that word, anguish, and Don got really quiet. After that it was like his defensiveness and anger evaporated, and it was just a matter of working out details. That was the closest I've felt to him since before the divorce."

From Karyn's point of view, once she gathered the courage to talk to both parents about her wish to live with her mother, her parents listened to her, got together, and came to an adult agreement that met her needs. Her parents made sure that she was not aware of the soul-searching her father went through, the patient, low-key, but persistent steps her mother took, or the emotionally wrenching mediation they were willing to go through to find a solution that took her needs and theirs into account. They refused to burden her with their adult problems. That let her get on with the crucial business of growing up.

Karyn is only one of many children and young adults I know who are growing up happily and well despite having lived through their parents' divorce. Neither they nor their parents have had an easy time of it. Most of the children and all of the parents I have talked to remember lonely, sad, fearful, and angry times. Karyn's eyes flashed when I asked her if she ever wished her parents had never divorced. "Of course it would be nice to have parents that were together." Then, with surprising and recently gained perspective, she added, "But I've never wished that my parents, being who they are, stayed together, because that would be awful, they couldn't get along."

Where did that perspective come from, that comfort with herself that allows Karyn to respect her parent's needs? Having seen some of that same self-acceptance and caring in many children of different ages, I am convinced that much of it is based upon how these children have seen their parents act, year after year, in good times and in bad.

While Karyn was living with her father, for example, she never heard him criticizing or attacking her mother. Don was deeply angry at Joan for the breakup and for shifting so much of the child-rearing responsibility to him while she went back to school and started her career. There were times when he confronted Joan, and there were times when he kept his anger to himself, but he was determined not to burden Karyn's life with these feelings. "I knew damn well that Karyn loved both of us, and it wasn't hard to figure out that putting her mother down or fighting in front of her would pull her apart." Karyn corroborates her parents' sensitiveness gratefully: "They never argue. I never remember them arguing. I don't think they've ever talked seriously bad about each other. They've never been like that."

What Karyn did see, the scenes now tucked away in the depths of her unconscious mind, were the hundreds of times when her parents talked comfortably to each other while picking her up or dropping her off, the lunch-time meetings where her parents handled the "business" of joint parenting, the shared Christmases that she pleaded for when she was little, which her parents continued even when both were remarried, and which she continues to cherish so much.

What Karyn heard, the words and phrases long-since blurred, were the sounds of caring, the listening, the willingness to face and solve problems. These patterns are indelibly recorded. "My mom is easy to talk to. She's quiet, so she's a good listener. But once she knows there's a problem, she'll keep bringing it up until it gets solved. And my dad really knows how to get things done, how to get other people to listen."

What Karyn absorbed, soaked in, learned at the deepest levels, was what kind of people both of her parents were, how they approached her, each other, their lives, day after day. She would have lost half this treasure if one parent had been forced out of her life; she might have lost all of it had her parents fought each other for her loyalty and love.

"Don has a wonderfully strong sense of himself," Joan says. "He is very bright and very accomplished. He knows how to negotiate in the world, and he feels that he can do anything he sets his mind to. He's also a lot more playful than I am. Karyn has picked this up. She has that same self-confidence and that same sense of fun."

At the same time, Karyn adds, "I've learned different things from both of them. Like from my mom, the way I talk to people and listen to them."

The many things that Karyn's parents did so well have made up, over the years, for the losses, insecurities, and hurts that their divorce caused. "When I was really little," Karyn described, "I hardly even remember seeing my mom. It seems like I didn't see her that much for a while after they split up. Then I hated it when she was with Peter. Then when my dad and my stepmom split up, it was very hard all over again. A lot of things seemed hard to me. *It's funny, like I look back and there have been a lot of hard things in my life, a lot of bad things that happened all along. But when I look at it overall, it's weird, but I think I've been really happy. It seems like I've had a really good life.*"

Karyn grew up in a divorced family with the same kind of feelings, divisions, and problems that can and do blacken years of children's lives. Her family, however, emphasized people against problems, not people against each other. Taking responsibility, really listening, clear communication, and win-win problem solving were integral parts of the fabric of her life. To her there is nothing extraordinary about these ideas; they are not methods or techniques, but natural ways of getting along in the world.

For some of us, the knowledge and skills that have become second nature to Karyn and her parents may seem new, difficult, even unworkable. If you are extremely hurt, angry, or fearful, at the end of your financial or personal resources, your negative feelings may be so strong that you cannot see any positive choices. If you are dealing with an extremely unreliable, unstable, manipulative, or hostile ex-spouse, you may be forced to fight for your own or your child's existence. Win-win thinking can not solve every problem or work in every situation. But for the majority of divorcing parents, consistent application of these concepts can produce realistic, livable, fair, and healthy outcomes for all concerned.

Rearing children is a difficult and challenging task certainly made no easier by divorce. This long and demanding undertaking becomes nearly impossible if separation and divorce are allowed to lead to endless fear, anger, and conflict. Parents have the power to guide this endeavor in either direction, to arm anger and hatred with words and weapons, or instead to empower their own better judgment, to improve their own lives and those of their children, in part by making the ideas in this book their own and putting them to work.

At the end of our talk, I asked Karyn to put into words what children in the midst of a divorce might not be able to tell their own parents. Here is her answer.

I'd say to think about your kids because they are the most important thing. Your kids are a lot smarter than you think and they pick up a lot more than you realize. Maybe your husband has left you for another woman and it hurts, or your wife is a real bitch, but every time you say something to your kids, you are just totally destroying them. Maybe your kids won't say anything, maybe they'll go away, but they will remember it. I know that divorce hurts adults a lot, but a lot of them get so caught up in their own self-pity. They don't realize they are really hurting their own kids.

I heard one of Mom's friends saying that she didn't want her kids to see their father. I think that's ridiculous. Kids need both their parents. Without both of them, I think a kid would grow up really messed up. Each parent has something to give and it's hard for the other one to see that when they are getting divorced.

The main thing is to think about the kids.

Appendix I
Where You Stand:
A Self-help Checklist for Parents

This checklist can help you to specify the challenges you and your ex-spouse face, and the resources you can bring to bear, in resolving child custody and related issues:

INSTRUCTIONS:

1. Answer as many questions as you can as honestly as you can. The more accurate you are, the more useful this information will be to you.

2. Complete all five sections.

3. If you cannot answer a question because of lack of information, or if the question is not appropriate to your situation, leave it blank.

4. This information is for your own use. You will probably find it easier to be fully honest if you plan not to let anyone else see your answers.

5. You may find yourself giving reasons or making excuses for your own or your ex-spouse's behavior. "I would be willing to share decision making about the children, but my ex-spouse just can't be trusted." Answer each question on the basis of what actually happens, not what you might do if things were different.

6. Be especially thoughtful in answering questions marked with an asterisk (*). These issues and how they are handled often impact very strongly on both the process and outcome of custody determination.

PART A: HOW YOU SEE YOUR EX-SPOUSE AS A PARENT

		YES	NO
1.	Our children need ongoing contact with him/her.	Y	N
2.	He/she seeks ongoing contact with the children.	Y	N
3.	He/she gives the children enough love and affection.	Y	N
4.	He/she provides the children with appropriate guidance and discipline.	Y	N
5.	Our children accept love and affection from him/her.	Y	N
6.	Our children accept guidance and discipline from him/her.	Y	N
7.	Our children communicate comfortably with him/her.	Y	N
8.	He/she communicates well with our children.	Y	N
9.	He/she is aware of and meets our children's basic physical and emotional needs.	Y	N
10.	He/she demonstrates ongoing commitment to our children's well-being.	Y	N
11.	He/she supports and fosters our children's contact with caring relatives.	Y	N
12.	He/she supports and fosters our children's contact with appropriate friends and playmates.	Y	N
13.	He/she supports and fosters our children's age-appropriate development and education.	Y	N
14.	He/she provides or arranges for adequate food, clothing, shelter, and medical care.	Y	N
15.	He/she spends adequate time with our children.	Y	N
16.	He/she provides adequate care for the children when at work or away.	Y	N
17.	He/she shows awareness of and sensitivity to our children's individual needs.	Y	N

18. He/she follows through on promises to or con-
    cerning the children.   Y   N
19. He/she demonstrates stable moods and reliable
    behavior towards or around our children.   Y   N
20. He/she is an adequate role model for our
    children.   Y   N
21.* He/she is physically abusive towards our
    children.   Y   N
22.* He/she is emotionally abusive towards our
    children.   Y   N
23.* He/she is sexually abusive towards our
    children.   Y   N
24.* He/she seriously neglects or endangers our
    children.   Y   N
25.* Alcoholism, drug abuse, or severe emotional
    problems seriously impair his/her motivation
    or ability to parent adequately.   Y   N

PART B: HOW YOU SEE YOURSELF ACTING AS A PARENT

		YES	NO
1.	Our children need ongoing contact with me.	Y	N
2.	I seek ongoing contact with our children.	Y	N
3.	I give our children adequate love and affection.	Y	N
4.	I give our children appropriate guidance and discipline.	Y	N
5.	Our children accept love and affection from me.	Y	N
6.	Our children accept guidance and discipline from me.	Y	N
7.	Our children communicate comfortably with me.	Y	N
8.	I communicate well with our children.	Y	N
9.	I am aware of and meet our children's basic physical and emotional needs.	Y	N
10.	I demonstrate an ongoing commitment to our children's well-being.	Y	N

11. I support and foster our children's contact with caring relatives. Y N
12. I support and foster our children's contact with appropriate friends and playmates. Y N
13. I support and foster our children's age-appropriate development and education. Y N
14. I provide or arrange for adequate food, clothing, shelter, and medical care for our children. Y N
15. I spend adequate time with our children. Y N
16. I provide adequate care for our children when I am at work or away. Y N
17. I am aware of and show sensitivity to our children's individual needs. Y N
18. I consistently follow through on promises to or concerning our children. Y N
19. I demonstrate stable moods and reliable behavior towards or around our children. Y N
20. I am an adequate role model for our children. Y N
21.* At times I am physically abusive towards our children. Y N
22.* At times I am emotionally abusive towards our children. Y N
23.* I have been sexually abusive towards our children. Y N
24.* I have seriously neglected or endangered our children. Y N
25.* Alcoholism, drug abuse, or severe emotional problems seriously impair my motivation or ability to parent adequately. Y N

PART C: HOW YOU SEE YOUR EX-SPOUSE ACTING TOWARDS YOU AS A PARENT

YES NO

1. He/she values my relationship with the children. Y N

2. He/she supports and fosters my relationship with our children. Y N

3. He/she seeks to maintain good communication with me concerning the children. Y N

4. He/she seeks a positive or businesslike relationship with me concerning the children. Y N

5. He/she shows adequate flexibility when dealing with me concerning the children. Y N

6. He/she plans to remain geographically close. Y N

7. He/she is willing to share decision making on important issues concerning the children. Y N

8. He/she is willing to compromise when it benefits the children. Y N

9. He/she makes a point of keeping me informed of important events concerning the children Y N

10. He/she follows through on specific agreements concerning the children. Y N

11. He/she lives up to agreed-upon and court-ordered responsibilities concerning the children. Y N

12. He/she speaks positively about me to the children. Y N

13. He/she acts civilly towards me in front of the children. Y N

14.* He/she consistently resists or blocks my communication or contact with the children. Y N

15.* He/she consistently criticizes or berates me in front of the children. Y N

16.* He/she consistently provokes or manipulates me to look bad in front of the children. Y N

17.* He/she is or has been physically abusive to me. Y N

18.* He/she is or has been psychologically abusive to me. Y N

19.* He/she threatens or has injured me physically or through financial manipulation, slander, child stealing, etc. Y N

20.* His/her primary motivation towards me seems
    to be hostility, vengeance, or power.   Y   N

PART D: HOW YOU SEE YOURSELF ACTING TOWARDS YOUR EX-SPOUSE

		YES	NO
1.	I value his/her relationship with our children.	Y	N
2.	I support and foster his/her relationship with our children.	Y	N
3.	I seek to maintain good communication with him/her concerning the children.	Y	N
4.	I seek a positive or businesslike relationship with him/her concerning the children.	Y	N
5.	I show adequate flexibility when dealing with him/her concerning the children.	Y	N
6.	I plan to remain geographically close.	Y	N
7.	I am willing to share decision making on important issues concerning the children.	Y	N
8.	I am willing to compromise when it benefits the children.	Y	N
9.	I make a point of keeping him/her informed of important events concerning the children.	Y	N
10.	I follow through on specific agreements concerning the children.	Y	N
11.	I live up to agreed-upon and court-ordered responsibilities concerning the children.	Y	N
12.	I speak positively about him/her to the children.	Y	N
13.	I act civilly towards him/her in front of the children.	Y	N
14.*	I consistently resist or block his/her communication or contact with the children.	Y	N
15.*	I consistently criticize or berate him/her in front of the children.	Y	N
16.*	I consistently provoke or manipulate to make him/her look bad in front of the children.	Y	N

17.* I am or have been physically abusive to
    him/her.   Y   N
18.* I am or have been psychologically abusive to
    him/her.   Y   N
19.* I threaten or have injured him/her physically
    or through financial manipulation, slander,
    child stealing, etc.   Y   N
20.* My primary motivation towards him/her
    seems to be hostility, vengeance, or power.   Y   N

PART E: RELATIONSHIP HISTORY

                                                        YES NO

1.* Our marital relationship was highly stressful
    (for example, frequent provocation, infidelity,
    threats, fighting, or violence).   Y   N
2.* Our relationship was ambivalent—we were
    strongly attracted to each other, but
    also very different. "We can't live with each
    other and we can't live without each other."   Y   N
3.* Our marriage ended traumatically (for exam-
    ple, with one or both of us feeling plotted
    against or abandoned; or after an explosive,
    violent fight).   Y   N
4.* Our relationship was damaged by alcoholism,
    drug abuse, or severe emotional disturbance in
    one or both of us.   Y   N
5.* We have had violent physical fights.   Y   N
6.* One or both of us have made allegations of
    physical or sexual abuse of the children.   Y   N
7.* One or both of us have taken and kept the
    children away from the other without his/her
    knowledge or permission (child stealing).   Y   N
8.* An influential third party (for example, a
    grandparent, a new mate, an influential friend,
    a lawyer, or a counselor) is making the situa-
    tion much worse.   Y   N

9.* We live, or are likely to be living, far apart.   Y   N
10.* One or both of us is in extremely difficult
     financial circumstances.   Y   N

PART F: JOINT RESOURCES

	YES	NO
1. Our marital relationship was characterized by mutual respect.	Y	N
2. Our separation was a mutual decision, arrived at after sufficient thought and discussion.	Y	N
3. Despite our differences, we have continued to put the children's needs first.	Y	N
4. We respect each other as parents.	Y	N
5. We trust each other as parents.	Y	N
6. We agree on basic values concerning the children.	Y	N
7. We have adequate financial resources.	Y	N
8. We have adequate personal resources (supportive friends, family, access to counseling).	Y	N
9. We are both relatively stable and well-functioning adults.	Y	N
10. We are able to communicate adequately concerning the children.	Y	N
11. We both plan to remain in the same geographical area.	Y	N
12. We are committed to resolving our differences in a constructive way.	Y	N
13. We each have or will be able to get adequate information about the laws governing divorce and child custody.	Y	N
14. We each have or will be able to get comprehensive information about our finances—income, expenses, debts, real estate, investments, inheritance, business, retirement, and taxes.	Y	N

15. When it comes to working things out or nego-
    tiating, we both seem to have about equal
    power.   Y   N
16. We both want a solution that is realistic and fair. Y   N

SCORING AND INTERPRETING YOUR ANSWERS:

PART A: HOW YOU SEE YOUR EX-SPOUSE AS A PARENT

RESOURCES: Add up the total number of "YES" answers
to items one through twenty.

16-20:   Despite your differences, you continue to see your ex-
         spouse in a positive light as a parent. If other areas are
         equally encouraging, you may be able to negotiate your
         custody agreement with relatively little outside help.
11-15:   Your view of your ex-spouse as a parent is qualified.
         You may have concerns about his or her motivation or
         ability to be a good parent that will make a joint
         solution harder to reach. Look at the items you have
         marked "NO" to evaluate (a) how important they are
         to you, and (b) how effectively you can communicate
         with your ex-spouse about them. Mediation may be
         very helpful for you.
6-10:   You have many significant concerns about your ex-
         spouse as a parent. To the extent that your concerns are
         legitimate, steps need to be taken so that you can feel
         better about him or her as a parent before negotiations
         are likely to succeed. It is possible that your view of
         your ex-spouse may be biased by feelings stemming
         from your couple relationship. If at one time you felt
         that he or she was a good or at least an adequate parent,
         but now see things in a dramatically different way, then
         your own feelings and perceptions, rather than his or
         her parental behavior, may require reevaluation. Medi-
         ation, family-oriented legal help, and counseling may
         be needed.

0-5:   You have a very negative view of your ex-spouse as a
        parent. He or she may be seriously deficient in parent-
        ing motivation or skills. Alternatively, your percep-
        tions in this area may be strongly colored by
        relationship issues. It is likely that the two of you will
        need a great deal of help from many sources to reach a
        fair and realistic custody agreement.

PROBLEM AREAS: A "YES" answer to any of items 21
through 25 indicates the presence of a serious problem that will
almost certainly need to be resolved before a satisfactory parenting plan can be pieced together. You and your ex-spouse may
benefit from counseling, legal advice, and representation as
steps towards improved communication and an eventual agreement.

PART B: HOW YOU SEE YOURSELF ACTING AS A PARENT

RESOURCES: Add up your "YES" responses to items 1
through 20.

16-20: You see yourself as a well-functioning parent. If your
        spouse shares this view, the two of you have many of
        the basic ingredients for working out a parenting
        agreement with minimal help.

11-15: You recognize some problems in your current func-
        tioning as a parent. Although these concerns may or
        may not become issues in working towards a custody
        agreement, your awareness of them is encouraging.
        You might consider counseling, family therapy, or a
        parenting class as positive steps to take. Mediation
        may be a useful forum for you and your ex-spouse.

6-10:   You see significant problems in your relationship with
        your children. These problems are likely to be impor-
        tant factors in working out a custody solution. Con-
        crete steps to deal with the specific problems you are
        experiencing should be taken as soon as possible.

These steps need to be made in the context of sound legal advice and, if possible, mediation.

0-5:   Your assessment of your relationship with your children is negative. Individual counseling or family therapy may well be needed to lay the groundwork for subsequent steps towards a successful parenting agreement.

PROBLEM AREAS: "YES" answers to any of items 21 through 25 indicate that you are aware of a serious problem area in your parenting. Specific help in these areas (for example, through individual or family therapy) is indicated. A supportive relationship with a skilled attorney may be vital for building the groundwork for later steps towards an agreement.

PART C: HOW YOU SEE YOUR EX-SPOUSE ACTING TOWARDS YOU AS A PARENT

RESOURCES: Add your total "YES" answers on items 1 through 13.

10-13:   You see your ex-spouse acting responsibly and respectfully towards you as a parent. To the extent that you are reciprocating this level of cooperation, the two of you are likely to be able to work out a custody agreement with relatively little outside help.

7-9:   Your ex-spouse appears to be dealing with you moderately well as a parent. Mediation may be a useful means of improving the level of cooperation and reaching a parenting agreement.

4-6:   You see your ex-spouse acting towards you in ways that make cooperation difficult. Counseling, family therapy, sound legal assistance, and mediation may all be useful in moving your situation forward.

0-3:   You find few positives and many negatives in the way your ex-spouse is dealing with you as a parent. Much work needs to be done to improve the situation. Individual or family therapy along with thoughtful legal advice and advocacy may be needed.

PROBLEM AREAS: Any "YES" answers on items 14 through 20 indicate serious problems in the relationship between you and your ex-spouse. These specific problems need to be addressed to work towards an optimal custody solution. Help from all of the sources mentioned above may be needed.

PART D: HOW YOU SEE YOURSELF ACTING TOWARDS YOUR EX-SPOUSE

RESOURCES: Add up your "Yes" responses to items 1 through 20.

16-20: You see yourself acting reliably and supportively towards your ex-spouse as a parent. If accurate, this conduct is an important resource.

11-15: You rate yourself as acting fairly cooperatively towards your ex-spouse. Specific problem areas may need to be improved as part of your work towards a custody solution.

6-10: Whatever your reasons, your ratings indicate that you are acting towards your spouse in a noncooperative way. Your behavior is likely to be part of the problem; a realistic and fair solution probably will require changes in how you perceive and deal with your ex-spouse.

0-5: Your actions towards your ex-spouse are indicative of severe problems in that relationship. The two of you will probably need extensive support, guidance, and help from others to work out a viable custody solution.

PART E: RELATIONSHIP HISTORY

One or more "YES" answers indicates that aspects of your history or current situation are frequently associated with difficulties in working out custody solutions. The specific problems you noted need to be addressed through appropriate means— individual or family therapy, drug or alcoholism treatment, vocational rehabilitation, or mediation—as vital early steps towards a successful custody arrangement.

PART F: JOINT RESOURCES

Add up your "YES" responses to items 1 through 16.

13-16: You and your ex-spouse have most of the resources needed to negotiate your own custody agreement with minimal help.

9-12: The two of you have many of the resources you need. If you can work together to change your "NO" responses to "YES," you have a good chance to come to a satisfactory agreement. Legal advice and mediation may be very useful to you.

5-8: You and your ex-spouse are missing many of the ingredients that would help you solve your custody problems. It will not be easy to agree on what the problems are or on how to address them. Individual or family therapy, legal advice and guidance, along with mediation may be useful steps.

0-4: You and your ex-spouse currently have few of the resources needed to work out custody problems cooperatively. You may need to work hard with the help of therapy, mediation, and legal assistance to stabilize your situations, build trust, regain respect for each other, and improve communication to the point that constructive solutions can be found.

SUMMARY:

Based on your scores and their interpretations, answer the following questions:

1. My view of my ex-spouse as a parent is
   A. positive—a resource.
   B. moderately positive—needs minor improvement.
   C. moderately negative—needs significant improvement.
   D. negative—an urgent problem.
2. If moderately or strongly negative, my view is based on
   A. long-term deficiencies in my ex-spouse as a parent.
   B. parenting problems related more to current stress and changes than to long-term deficiencies.

   C. dramatic changes in my view of him or her because of what happened between us in the course of our separation and divorce.

3. My assessment of myself as a parent right now is
   A. positive—a resource.
   B. moderately positive—needs minor improvement.
   C. moderately negative—needs significant improvement.
   D. negative—an urgent problem.

4. Five steps I can take right now or in the immediate future to improve my functioning as a parent are the following:

5. My ex-spouse is acting towards me as a parent
   A. supportively—a resource.
   B. moderately well—needs minor improvement.
   C. not well—needs significant improvement.
   D. destructively—an urgent problem.

6. I am acting towards my ex-spouse as a parent
   A. supportively—a resource.
   B. moderately well—needs minor improvement.
   C. not well—needs significant improvement.
   D. destructively—an urgent problem.

7. The history of our relationship and situation is
   A. relatively positive—a resource.
   B. moderately positive—some troublesome areas.
   C. moderately negative—at risk for further problems; need a different approach.
   D. negative—an urgent problem.

8. When I compare our resources to our problem areas, I believe
   A. we can work out a good agreement with minimal help.
   B. we can work out an agreement, but that help will be needed in one or more areas.
   C. significant help is needed in a variety of areas.
   D. our problems are severe compared to our apparent resources. We are likely to need legal advice and guidance, individual or family therapy, or other specific help in addressing our custody situation to meet our own and our children's needs.

9. Steps I can take individually or with my ex-spouse to address the problems I have identified are the following:

Appendix II
Age-appropriate Schedules

There are as many good schedules for children as there are separated couples who are able to cooperate when it comes to parenting; every successfully restructured family works out a unique schedule that makes sense for the children and parents.

Working out a time-sharing solution for your family is a matter of balance. Your children's need for stability and predictability of schedule must at times be balanced against the overriding necessity for a resolution of parental conflict. Their need for frequent and continuing contact with both parents may have to be balanced against the complexities and demands of everyone's schedules. The needs and capacities of an older child may have to be balanced against those of a younger one.

The following schedules represent guidelines for children of different ages.

Early Infancy—Birth to Six Months

Developmental tasks:
    Physiological stabilization.
    Bonding and attachment to one or more parental figures.
What's important:
    Basic caretaking and nurturing—feeding and diapering, but also being talked to, played with, *held,* and cuddled.
    Continuity and consistency of care.
    Responsive caretakers.
    Small number of caretakers.
    Smooth, predictable routines.
    Stability of caretaking setting(s).
    Shorter, more frequent periods of time with a noncustodial parent, rather than longer contacts farther apart.

(Overnight visits with a noncustodial parent are probably *not* in the infant's best interests.)

Separation from either parent no longer than a few days.

What to watch out for:

Excessive fretfulness and crying.

Sleeping, eating, and digestive problems.

Failure to gain weight and thrive.

Unresponsiveness or apathy.

Major upsets when exposed to different caretakers or environments.

Some possible parenting plans:

1. One primary home. The other parent spends two or three hours, two or three times per week with the child; becomes primary caretaker one weekend day per week.

2. One primary home. The other parent spends two or three hours, two or three times per week with the child; becomes primary caretaker for a twenty-four-hour stretch once a week.

3. One primary home supplemented by high quality day care (no more than four infants per adult). Other parent spends two or three hours, two or three times each week with the child.

What to do if problems arise:

Take quick, cooperative action.

Consult your pediatrician.

Cooperate in observing the infant in its different environments, searching for the key to the problem. Remember, the problem may not be "going up and back," but may be too many caretakers, an impaired caretaker, an unsuitable environment (e.g., too noisy, too chaotic), food allergies, etc.

Later Infancy—Six Months to Eighteen Months

Developmental tasks:

Deepening of loving attachments to caretakers.

Development of basic trust and security.

Exploring the environment from a secure base.

What's important:
Basic caretaking and nurturing.
Continuity and consistency of care.
Small number of responsive caretakers.
Predictability and familiarity.
A safe environment.
Stability of caretaking settings.
Contact periods according to the following schedules:
(a) If the infant is well attached to both parents, then
    contacts can be longer, spaced no longer than two or
    three days apart.
(b) If the infant is not familiar with one parent, caretaking
    periods by that parent should be short and frequent, as
    with a younger infant.
(c) Try to match schedules to the child's temperament. An
    easy child can handle longer times away from each
    parent and a more flexible schedule; a slow-to-warm-up
    child may need to stay with frequent, short contacts
    until older; a difficult child may require even shorter
    visits on a very predictable schedule.
(d) Overnight stays are still likely to be stressful to
    the child. An easy and adaptable child with moti-
    vated and cooperative parents may handle them well,
    but other infants in less ideal circumstances will
    probably do better if overnights are not started this
    early.
What to watch out for:
Excessive fretfulness and crying.
Excessive lethargy or listlessness.
Sleeping, eating, and digestive problems.
Failure to thrive.
Fearful reactions. (Negative reactions to strangers are
    normal during this time, but similar reactions to a
    parent, or indifference, may indicate attachment
    problems).
Delayed development of walking and speech.
Night terrors and regression (i.e., caused by abandonment
    by a parent after bonding has taken place).

Some possible parenting plans:
1. One primary home. The other parent spends from two hours to a day, two to three times per week with the child.
2. One primary home. The other parent has the child as above, but with one overnight per week.
3. One primary home plus high quality day care. Schedule as in 1.
4. Two homes, although the child spends significantly more time at one of them and no more than two overnights per week at the other. This arrangement should be considered only for mature, adjustable children and very cooperative parents.

What to do if problems arise:
Take quick, cooperative action.

Consult your pediatrician, other child specialists if needed.

Watch the child closely in its different environments. The problem may be insufficient familiarity with a caretaker, an unsafe or otherwise unsuitable environment, or simply slower development of enough security to allow separation from a primary parent.

Toddlers—Eighteen Months to Three Years

Developmental tasks:
Becoming an individual.

Autonomy.

Safe separation from parents.

What's important:
Firm support—parents need to set firm limits *and* allow freedom to explore.

Secure, patient, and firm parents and caretakers.

During the "terrible two's" parents need to allow the child to resist on unimportant issues, but must stand firm when it comes to safety, self-control, and interacting with others.

Attentive monitoring and parenting.

Verbal explanations and reassurance, repeated over and
over.

Close, consistent, frequent contact with both parents
according to the following schedules:

(a) Longer stays, entire days or overnights, spaced up to
three or even four days apart, can be handled by
secure, well-adjusted children towards the end of this
age range.

(b) Entire weekends away from home base may still be too
much for children this age.

(c) Less adaptable children, or those still not familiar with
a parent, may still need shorter, more frequent
contacts.

What to watch out for:

Regression.

Developmental lags (e.g., in speech, play, motor control).

Severe separation fears.

Excessive masturbation.

Excessive aggression.

Frequent, severe tantrums.

Some possible parenting plans:

1. One primary home. The other parent has the child
during the days up to three times per week, on a
predictable schedule.

2. One primary home. The other parent has the child as
above, but with one overnight per week.

3. One primary home plus good day care. Schedule as in 1
or 2 above.

4. Two homes, with the child spending somewhat more
time in one than the other. Two or three overnights
spaced regularly throughout the week.

What to do if problems arise:

Consult and problem-solve cooperatively.

Compare notes with other parents—the problem may be a
normal developmental phase.

Observe the child carefully. He or she may need more time
to form a secure, primary attachment, may need firmer

boundaries, more permission to explore, more
predictability, more explanation and reassurance.
Consult with a pediatrician, other specialists as needed.

Preschoolers—Three Years through Five Years

Developmental tasks:
Development of initiative.
Impulse management.
Sex role identification.
Peer relationships.
What's important:
Clear parental roles and values.
Parental cooperation. (These children react strongly to
parental conflict.)
Frequent and continuing contact with the same-sex parent.
(A child this age should *not* be encouraged to feel that
he or she has driven away the same-sex parent, and that
he or she now has a unique relationship with the
opposite-sex parent.)
Frequent and predictable contacts. (Predictability of schedules
is at least as important as frequency or duration.)
Reassurance of love and support, that the divorce is not
their fault, that they don't have the power to undo it.
Access to nursery school or other settings for stimulation
and socialization.
Special contact considerations as follows:
(a) Even during holiday periods, children this age should
not go longer than one week without contact with a
parent.
(b) Supplement longer separations with phone calls.
What to watch out for:
Withdrawal and depression—loss of normal cheerfulness
and curiosity.
Eating or sleeping disturbances.
Crying for long periods after leaving one parent.
Delay in toilet training.

Regression—loss of previously gained skills.

Extreme neediness—demanding to sleep with a parent.

Overly compliant behavior—too serious, emotionally constricted, too "good."

Some possible parenting plans:

1. Two or three nights at one home, spaced throughout the week, the remaining time at the other home.
2. Same as above, but supplemented by good day care.
3. Three consecutive days and nights with one parent, four with the other.
4. One week with one parent, the next with the other.

What to do if problems arise:

Listen to your child; he or she may be able to tell you just what is wrong.

Examine the parent-parent relationship; your child may be sensing and amplifying your conflicts.

What roles is the child playing? A child who has become a substitute adult may be loaded with guilt and anger.

Can the child's schedule be made more regular and predictable?

Reassure the child frequently and clearly of your love.

School-age Children—Six to Twelve

Developmental tasks:

Free energy from family concerns in order to experience friends, school, learning, industry, and cooperative play.

Gain a sense of personal competence and self-esteem.

Develop logical thought applied to concrete objects.

Develop a sense of fairness.

What's important:

Enough stability and security at home to allow full involvement outside the home.

A reasonably well-structured schedule with some flexibility.

Exclusion from parents' conflicts and insulation from their

negative views of each other. (These children, especially the older ones, suffer intensely when they feel they have to choose between their parents. They may respond with intense anger or by rejecting one parent completely.)

Lots of explanation, discussion, being talked to and listened to.

Geographical proximity and continuity of school and friends. (An ideal arrangement for the child is when both parents continue to live in the same area.)

Flexibility. (This becomes important as these children develop strong friendships and activities outside the home. Parental insistence on a planned contact at the expense of a much-desired activity can generate resentment.)

Contact schedules as follows:

(a) Spontaneous contacts. (A parent's dropping in on the child, or the child's initiating a contact with a parent, can be valuable as long as such contacts do not stir up parental conflict.)

(b) Particularly for younger school-age children, two weeks without contact with a parent is too long. Longer separations should be supplemented by brief contacts, spontaneous visits, and phone calls.

What to watch out for:

Increased anxiety, restlessness, overactivity.

Increased moodiness, tantrums, aggression.

School problems.

Childhood depression—unhappiness, intense fears, feelings of rejection, sleep problems. (In older children, depression is shown through withdrawal, sadness, grief, yearning for an absent parent.)

Denial of all problems—a bubbly front too good to be true.

Intense, one-sided anger at the parent who is blamed for the divorce. (This can develop into absolute rejection of one parent.)

Overburdened children—being used as confidants by parents.

Some possible parenting plans:

If parental conflict is low, school-age children can do well with many different parenting plans, as long as they provide for relatively frequent and adequate contact with both parents.

1. Friday after school through Sunday evening or Monday morning, every other week, plus one or two overnights during the two-week stay with the other parent.
2. Three days with one parent, four days with the other.
3. Alternating weeks with each parent.
4. Alternate weekends with each parent, two or three days at each home during the week.
5. Three and a half days with each parent; weekends are also split.
6. Two weeks with each parent, with one or two midweek overnights with the other.
7. Older children may be able to handle even longer stays, if these are supplemented by phone calls and some contacts with the other parent.
8. Some parents find it manageable to have the child spend the school year at one home, with the bulk of vacation time spent at the other. Supplement contact with frequent and regular calls and visits.

What to do if problems arise:

Talk to and listen to your child.

Examine both parents' relationships with the child. Are you overburdening your child with adult roles?

Examine the parent-parent relationship. Is your child caught in a loyalty conflict?

Does the child's schedule provide enough structure and predictability?

Does the child's schedule provide for adequate flexibility and spontaneity?

Are geographic shifts disrupting your child's friendships and school involvements?

Is your child missing one or both parents too much because of too-long separations and inadequate contact?

Is your child confused because of a schedule that is too complex or unpredictable?

Teenagers—Thirteen through Eighteen

Developmental tasks:
Separation.
Peer involvement.
Development of own identity.
Sexual identity.
Independence.
What's important:
Emotional stability and maturity on the part of both parents.
Adequate, but flexible and age-appropriate parental controls.
Continuing, meaningful contact with both parents.
Schedules flexible enough to respect the teenager's need for involvement with peers and independent activities.
Low levels of parent-parent conflict.
Sensitivity to teenagers' need to be consulted, informed, and listened to without giving up the adult/child relationship.
Treating teenagers as individuals.
Awareness that teenagers do not need extended time with either parent.
What to watch out for:
Withdrawal from the family coupled with social isolation or involvement with antisocial activities or peers.
Intense feelings of loss, helplessness, low self-esteem, depression, suicidal thoughts or feelings.
Uncontrollable anger, violence towards a parent.
Promiscuous sexual involvements.
Manipulatively joining one parent in attacking the other.
School failure.
Substance abuse.

Some possible parenting plans:
1. Home base with one parent, a mixture of scheduled and spontaneous overnights, shorter visits, and outings with the other parent.
2. Children spend school year as above; during summer vacation and other long holidays, the situation is reversed.
3. For some teenagers, the more structured plans discussed for younger age groups may continue to work, particularly if the parents are geographically close.
4. Some families work out year-by-year arrangements with older children. These plans need to respect the teenager's needs for continuity in friendships and school placement, and should always be supplemented with telephone and other contacts as frequently as possible.

What to do if problems arise:
Listen to, talk to, and, as they become increasingly mature individuals, negotiate with teenagers.

Determine need for counseling or therapy for unhappy teenagers, who may be strongly resistive to it.

Parental cooperation in dealing with teenagers' problems is a necessity.

Persist in working with your child until you have a clear picture of his or her individual feelings, wants, and needs.

Other Scheduling Possibilities

Some parents have the children live in the family home; the parents move in and out on a fixed schedule.

Some schools divide the entire year into four relatively short grading periods separated by equal-length vacations. A child can spend each school period in one home, the vacations in the other. If the homes are close together, an older child may spend alternate school periods at each home.

Teenagers often want to try living with their up-till-now noncustodial parent. In many cases this arrangement can be a constructive change.

Holidays and Vacations

Holidays are extremely important as times of shared enjoyment, family tradition, and meaning. Restructured families living near each other can usually work out ways for the children to spend part of each important holiday at both homes. Families separated by too many miles for this arrangement usually work out ways of alternating important holidays each year.

Children of Different Ages

Except with infants and adolescents, it usually makes sense for all the children to share the same schedule. Having brothers and sisters along can be an important support for children. Babies have special needs that may well prevent a parent from being with both infants and older children simultaneously. Teenagers' needs for peer involvement and for controlling their own lives may place them on different schedules from their younger brothers and sisters as well.

Appendix III
Custody Laws in the United States (as of 1987)*

The laws relating to child custody and the manner in which they are applied vary greatly from state to state. In addition, custody laws are constantly changing through legislation and judicial decisions. Although the information in this appendix provides a general overview of relevant laws in each state, it is not meant as legal advice; *anyone involved in litigating or negotiating child custody should consult with a local attorney.*

Two important pieces of federal legislation impact on all of the states: the Parental Kidnapping Prevention Act (PKPA), and the Uniform Child Custody Jurisdiction Act (UCCJA). The PKPA gives the federal courts jurisdiction to resolve conflicting state custody decrees, to discourage parental kidnapping. Both the PKPA and the UCCJA provide that valid custody decrees issued in one state must be honored by another. The UCCJA has been adopted by all fifty states. State courts are applying it fairly consistently to decide which state has jurisdiction over a case, when that jurisdiction should be shifted, and even to deal more consistently with custody decrees from foreign countries.

The following discussion presents some of the key features of custody law in each of the fifty states, Washington, D.C., Puerto Rico, and the U.S. Virgin Islands. Please note that in some states, including New York, the absence of joint custody legisla-

---

*The summaries below are based on information in Jay Folberg, ed., *Joint Custody and Shared Parenting* (The Bureau of National Affairs, Inc., 1984); Doris J. Freed and Timothy B. Walker, "Family Law in the Fifty States: An Overview," *Family Law Quarterly, XIX,* 4, Winter 1986; Lenore J. Weitzman, *The Divorce Revolution* (New York: Macmillan, 1985); and *The Family Law Reporter* (The Bureau of National Affairs, Inc., 1987).

tion does not prevent parents from working out shared custody agreements that can be formalized by the court.

Alabama did not have joint custody statutes as of 1986. Its courts have generally resisted shared custody. The legal test for modification of custody is that the change would materially promote the child's best interests and welfare. The child's wishes are considered.

Alaska enacted joint custody laws in 1982 to assure both parents the opportunity to guide and nurture the child. Parental agreement is not required for the judge to consider joint custody. If one parent requests joint custody but it is denied, the judge must state the reasons on the record. Sole custody can be modified to joint custody at any time. Clear and convincing evidence must be shown to justify termination of visitation. The court can order mediation within 30 days after a child custody petition is filed. The court can appoint an attorney for the child. Grandparent visitation is allowed in custody disputes.

Arizona had no joint custody statute as of 1987. The courts have generally been supportive of shared custody. The court considers the child's preferences, parental wishes, and significant relationships. It can appoint an attorney for the child. Alternative dispute resolution through conciliation court is authorized. Before a custodial parent may remove the child from the state against the noncustodial parent's wishes, a hearing must be held to consider and balance the best interests of the child, the siblings, and the parents. Grandparents have been awarded custody even over parental objection.

Arkansas did not have statutory custody guidelines as of 1987. There is a provision for grandparent visitation.

California adopted strong joint custody laws in 1980 and has modified them since then. It is public policy to assure frequent and continuing contact with both parents. Joint custody is presumed when parents agree on it, but can be ordered even when parents disagree. One factor the court is to consider is which parent is more likely to allow the child frequent contact with the other—the so-called "friendly parent" or "better able to share" clause. If a parent's request for joint custody is denied, the court must state its reasons for denial. Sole custody may be modified to joint in accordance with certain standards. The court may not rely upon one parent's economic superiority in applying the best interests test. Mediation is mandatory. The court may order a custody investigation or appoint an attorney for the child. The child's wishes are considered. Visitation may be granted "to the noncustodial parent or any other person having an interest in the welfare of the child." Visitation is a right of the child, and should not be made contingent upon another duty, such as timely payment of child support.

Colorado's joint custody statute has been in place since 1983. Joint custody requires parental agreement, and even then the court must find it to be in the child's best interests, and does not need to state its reasons for denial. A parenting plan may be filed with the court. The court is to consider which parent is more likely to support the child's contact with the other. Sole custody can be modified to joint following statutory guidelines. Mediation or evaluation may be ordered. The child's wishes are to be considered. Visitation is seen as a child's right. An attorney for the child may be appointed. The law provides for grandparent visitation.

Connecticut law has defined joint custody since 1982. The court may not order joint custody without parental agreement, but can order conciliation to that end. If parents agree on joint custody and submit a fair and equitable plan, that plan shall be incorporated into the court's decree. The court must write its reasons for denial of joint custody. Custody may be modified for compelling reasons, but under a "preponderance of evidence" test. The child's wishes are considered, and the court may appoint an attorney for the child.

Delaware's definition of Joint Natural Custodians has been construed to give each parent equal powers and duties. The court has the option to order joint guardianship. Parental agreement is not required. The child's wishes are to be considered.

District of Columbia had no joint custody legislation as of 1987. The child's wishes are considered.

Florida enacted joint custody legislation in 1982. The court is directed to order shared custody unless it finds it detrimental to the child. Parental agreement is not required. The "friendly parent," that parent more likely to support the child's contact with the other, is considered, as are the child's preferences. Mediation is available.

Georgia courts have generally not favored shared custody. The divorcing party "not in default" is entitled to custody, but the court may look into all relevant circumstances of the parties. A child age 14 or older "shall have the right to select the parent with whom he desires to live," unless that parent is unfit. Custody agreements reached by parents may be ratified by the court if found to be in the child's best interests.

Hawaii enacted joint custody legislation in 1980. Although joint custody is not presumed, the court has the option of awarding it upon the application of either parent; parental agreement is not required. Sole custody may be modified to joint custody at any time. Joint legal custody can be awarded without joint physical custody. Joint custody may be modified or terminated upon the request of one parent or on the court's own motion. Either party can request the court to order an investigation to see if joint custody is appropriate. The wishes of the child are considered. Custody may be awarded to persons other than the parents if in the child's best interests.

Idaho passed joint custody legislation in 1982. Joint custody is presumed to be in a child's best interest unless there is a preponderance of evidence to the contrary. Parental agreement is not needed for an order of joint custody. The court must state its reasons for the denial of joint custody. The court can determine how the child's time is to be shared.

Illinois passed a joint custody law in 1982. Both parties must agree for joint custody to be ordered. An investigation may be ordered by the court. The child's wishes are considered, and the court may appoint an attorney for the child. The court does not need to state reasons for an initial joint custody order. Modification of custody within two years of a previous award requires a finding that the child's physical or emotional health is in danger. Modification or termination of joint custody may be requested by one parent or the court, but requires a finding based on clear and convincing evidence that a change has occurred. If parents agree to end joint custody, the court shall terminate it in the child's interests.

Indiana enacted joint custody legislation in 1983 and 1984. The parents' agreement on custody is a primary consideration, but need not determine the court's decision. Modification of custody requires a showing of detriment to the child. The wishes of the child are considered.

Iowa passed joint custody legislation early—in 1977. It is public policy to encourage frequent and continuing contact with both parents and equal parental access to information about the child. Joint custody may be awarded on the request of either parent, although "child's best interest" factors do not mandate a joint custody award. Sole custody can be modified to joint custody in accordance with statutory requirements. The court must write its reasons for denial of a joint custody

request. Mediation may be required. The child's preferences
are considered.

Kansas enacted joint custody legislation in 1979, in
general preferring it. The court may order joint custody on
the request of either parent, although the time spent in each
home is not specified. If joint custody is denied, the court
must state its reasons. Both parents individually or together
may submit a parenting plan prior to the court's decree. The
court shall consider a variety of factors including the history
of care and control of the child, the wishes of the child and
the parents, interaction with parents, siblings and others, and
the "willingness and ability of each parent to respect and
appreciate the bond between the child and the other parent."
Repeated denial or interference with visitation rights, or
repeated misuse of child support, may be considered a change
of circumstances justifying custody modification. Maternal
preference through the "tender years" presumption is
specifically abrogated.

Kentucky enacted legislation defining joint custody in
1980. The court retains the option to order joint or sole
custody in the child's best interests. When custody is
contested, the court can order an investigation. The court
may not consider conduct of a proposed custodian that does
not affect his relationship with the child. Leaving the family
residence to avoid physical harm may not be considered
abandonment. The child's wishes are considered. Grandparent
visitation is permitted if a parent is deceased.

Louisiana enacted joint custody laws in 1982. Joint
custody is presumed unless parents decide otherwise;
inability to cooperate rebuts the joint custody presumption.
The court shall order parents to submit a plan for
implementing a joint custody order. Any custody order may
be modified to joint custody. Joint custody may be modified
or ended upon petition of one or both parents or by the court's

own motion. The court can order an investigation; the wishes of the child are considered. The court must state its reasons for denial or modification of joint custody. Changes in custody require proof of imperative reasons, specifically a material change in circumstances.

Maine passed custody legislation in 1981. Joint custody is presumed if parents agree on it, but can be ordered if requested by only one parent. The court shall state its reasons for denial of joint custody requested by both parents. The court may appoint an attorney for the child; the wishes of the child are to be considered.

Maryland does not have joint custody statutes, but a detailed opinion by the attorney general has allowed joint custody. A judge may award joint custody on the request of one parent, although such an award may not be appropriate in the absence of shared parenting values or parental inability to communicate in the child's best interests. There is a provision for grandparent visitation.

Massachusetts passed joint custody legislation in 1983. Shared legal custody is presumed to be in the best interests of the child. Awards are permitted in accordance with parental agreement unless the court finds that the plan would not be in the child's best interest. Any form of custody can be modified to joint custody in accordance with statutes. The court may order an evaluation or appoint an attorney for the child. In the absence of misconduct, maternal and paternal rights are held as equal. Rights to a child's records are not altered by the custody decree. The law provides for grandparent visitation.

Michigan's joint custody laws, passed in 1980, are quite favorable to joint custody. Joint custody is presumed if parents agree, and may be ordered based on the request of either parent. The court must state on record reasons for granting or denying joint custody requested by one parent.

The court is directed to consider which parent is more supportive of the child's close and continuing relationship with the other parent. Mediation services are available. The child's wishes are considered; the court may appoint an attorney for the child. A disputed removal of a child from the state requires a hearing in which the best interests of the child, siblings, and parents shall be weighed. Grandparental visitation rights are broadly construed.

Minnesota enacted legislation preferring joint custody in 1981. The court has the option to order joint custody, but the parents' ability to cooperate is to be considered, and joint custody is not to be used to coerce cooperation. Mediation is available. The wishes of the child are considered. The law provides for grandparent visitation.

Mississippi passed joint custody laws in 1983. Joint custody is presumed if the parents agree, but may be ordered by the court on one parent's request. Sole custody may be modified to joint custody upon petition by both parents or upon one parent showing a material change in circumstances making the previous custody adverse to the child. The court may appoint an attorney for the child. Overnight visitation should not be restricted without proof of danger to the child.

Missouri's joint custody statutes were enacted in 1983. The court has the option to award joint custody, but the parties must submit a written plan for joint custody. The wishes of the child are considered. A parent's right of visitation may be qualified by the child's best interests.

Montana passed joint custody legislation in 1981. It is public policy to assure the child of frequent and continuing contact with both parents and to encourage parents to share rights and responsibilities. Parental agreement on joint custody is not required, and the court must write its reasons for denial of joint custody. Among other specified factors, the court shall consider which parent is more supportive of the child's contacts with the other parent. Custody preference shall not be based on sex. The court may direct the parties to consult with professionals to resolve controversy or formulate a parenting plan. Custody may be modified following strict statutory guidelines. A child's wishes are considered and an attorney may be appointed to represent the child. There is a provision for grandparent visitation.

Nebraska has a statute permitting joint custody when both parents agree. However, the state supreme court has declared that even in those cases the court must conduct a public hearing and apply the best interests test. It writes, "Such an award must be reserved for the most rare of cases." The children's wishes may be considered and an attorney for the children may be appointed.

Nevada legislated joint custody in 1981. Joint custody is presumed to be in the child's best interests if the parents have agreed, but may be ordered upon the request of one parent. If it is requested and denied, the court must write its reasons. Any custody order can be modified to joint custody. The court notes which parent is more supportive of the child's frequent and continuing contact with the other parent. Mediation is available. The wishes of the child are considered.

New Hampshire enacted joint custody laws in 1982. Joint custody is preferred; it may be ordered upon the request of one parent. Sole custody can be modified to joint custody following the best interests standard. If requested and denied, the court shall state its reasons. The child's wishes are considered. New Hampshire is one of two states in which the court must appoint a guardian ad litem (an independent legal representative) for the child if custody is contested.

New Jersey did not have joint custody legislation as of 1987. However, the court must consider a parental joint custody agreement. The wishes of the child are also considered. Grandparent visitation rights are strongly affirmed, as are a noncustodial parent's rights to exercise visitation without undue restrictions.

New Mexico enacted child custody legislation in 1981. Judicial interpretation has held that parental incompatibility does not support a joint custody arrangement. The court may order joint legal custody without joint physical custody. If a parental plan for joint custody is in the child's best interests, the court shall incorporate it into a provisional joint custody decree. The court may reject a plan found not to be in the child's best interests, but must state its reasons. If either party moves to terminate joint custody within 90 days, the court is required to do so. The court may terminate joint custody at any time if it determines that it is not in the child's best interest. The child's wishes are considered; an attorney for the child may be appointed.

New York had not enacted joint custody legislation as of 1987. However, the courts can ratify shared-parenting agreements. Case law has supported not awarding custody to a parent who degrades the other parent in the child's presence. Grandparental visitation may be granted if in the child's best interests. Disputed removal of a child from the state warrants a hearing to balance parental and children's rights. A change in custody requires a "heavy burden" of proof that it is in the child's best interests.

North Carolina enacted a form of joint custody in 1967. It provides that if it is clearly in the best interests of the child, the court can award custody to two or more persons. Case law has supported the wishes of the child. There are provisions for grandparent visitation.

North Dakota had not enacted joint custody legislation as of 1987. However, the courts have generally been favorable to it. The wishes of the child are considered.

Ohio has joint custody legislation dating to 1981. Parents seeking joint custody must submit a mutually agreed-upon plan. If joint custody is decided to be in the child's best interests, the court shall incorporate that plan into its provisional orders. If not deemed in the child's best interests, the court may reject it, although it must state its reasons. Provisional joint custody may be modified within 60 days, and must be terminated if either party so moves within 90 days. The child's wishes are considered; an attorney for the child may be appointed. Visitation rights may be modified without reference to the guidelines for custody modification.

Oklahoma enacted custody laws in 1983 that make joint custody and sole custody equally preferred. A parental plan is required, which the court may incorporate into its order as is or in modified form. The court may appoint an arbitrator to resolve disputes between joint custody parents; if a parent refuses to consent to arbitration, joint custody may be terminated. The child's wishes are considered.

Oregon's joint custody laws date to 1979. The court has the option to award joint custody, although case law bases this award on a request by both parents and their ability to cooperate. The best interests of the child are the primary consideration, and the child's wishes are a factor in this. Changes in the strength of a parent-child relationship may constitute a change in circumstances sufficient to support modification of custody. An attorney may be appointed for the child.

Pennsylvania passed joint custody legislation in 1982. It is public policy to assure reasonable and continuing contact with both parents and to encourage sharing of rights and responsibilities; case law has been supportive of this. Joint custody may be awarded on the request of one or both parents, or under a plan developed by them. If requested and denied, the court must state its reasons. The court considers which parent is more likely to support the child's continuing contact with the other. Willful interference with court-ordered visits may be punishable through contempt, but not through custody modification. The court may require parents to attend counseling and may consider the recommendations of counselors in awarding custody. Although both parents shall have access to all records of the child, the court shall not order disclosure of the address of a shelter for battered spouses. The law provides for grandparent visitation, even following stepparent adoption. Change in custody requires proof of a substantial change in circumstances.

Rhode Island did not have joint custody legislation as of 1987. An attorney may be appointed for the child in contested cases.

South Carolina had no joint custody legislation as of 1987. Concerning shared custody, the state supreme court has declared, "Divided custody is to be avoided if at all possible, and will be approved only under exceptional circumstances. Modification of custody requires demonstration of a material and substantial change of circumstances. A guardian ad litem (an independent legal representative) may be appointed for the child; parents are entitled to copies of the guardian's report and recommendations, and can cross-examine concerning it.

South Dakota had no joint custody legislation as of 1987. The penalty for parental child stealing has been increased. The child's wishes are considered. Grandparents have reasonable visitation rights if in child's best interests.

Tennessee did not have joint custody guidelines as of 1987. Case law indicates that the "tender years" doctrine—that a young child is presumed to need maternal care—is a factor that can be used in deciding between two fit parents. Grandparental visitation is supported by statute. The child's wishes are considered.

Texas enacted joint custody legislation in 1979, using the term "joint managing conservators" as contrasted to "possessive conservator." The parents' joint parenting plan shall be set forth in the court order unless the court finds it not in the child's best interests. In that case the court may request revised agreements or make its own orders. Case law emphasizes the requirement of parental agreement for joint conservators. The child's wishes are considered. Interference with a child custody order creates civil liability.

Utah had no joint custody laws as of 1987. An abandoned spouse is entitled to custody unless the court directs otherwise. Past parental conduct and moral standards shall be considered. The child's wishes may be considered and an attorney for the child may be appointed if custody is disputed. The court can override the parents' agreed-upon plan if it finds it not in the child's best interests. Appropriate cases may be referred to mediation programs where available, or referred for counseling. Visitation with grandparents or others may be granted if in the children's best interests and welfare. Maternal preference through the "tender years" doctrine has been deemed unconstitutional.

Vermont did not have joint custody legislation as of 1987. The child's wishes are considered. Stepparent custody is recognized by statute, as is grandparental visitation.

Virginia had no joint custody legislation as of 1987. In determining custody, the child's wishes are considered, along with other specified factors. Parental sex is not to be a factor. A leading case granted custody to a stepfather following abandonment by the child's natural mother, based on the child's best interests. Grandparents, siblings, and other parties with an interest in the child may be granted visitation. In general, visitation is not to be restricted without a showing of danger to the child.

Washington had not passed joint custody legislation as of 1987. Visitation with a noncustodial parent is seen as a child's right. The child's wishes are considered, and an attorney for the child may be appointed. The Interference with Custody Statute has been amended to include families with joint or shared custody; the penalty is a misdemeanor. Grandparents, siblings, and other persons with an interest in a child have visitation rights.

West Virginia had no joint custody statutes as of 1987. The child's wishes are considered. The child's primary caretaker is favored for custody if he or she meets the minimum standards for a fit parent.

Wisconsin enacted joint custody legislation in 1977. Joint custody is permitted if parties agree. Custody may be modified if found to be in the best interests of the child. The child's wishes are considered. Case law indicates that a parent must be granted custody over a third party (e.g., grandparent) unless the parent is unfit, unable to care for the child, or for some other compelling reason. Spousal abuse must be considered in determining custody. Wisconsin is one of two states in which a guardian ad litem (an independent legal representative) must be appointed for the child if custody is disputed. There is a provision for grandparent visitation.

Wyoming had not enacted joint custody legislation as of 1987. The child's wishes are considered. Custody may be modified if the change is in the child's best interests. The state supreme court has decided that the court deciding custody must make specific findings concerning the parents' abilities to cooperate, the child's interaction with the parents and significant others, and the geographical proximity of the parents. Grandparental visitation rights are specified by statute.

Puerto Rico had not enacted joint custody legislation as of 1987. The child's wishes are considered.

Virgin Islands had no joint custody legislation as of 1987. The child's wishes are considered.

Stages of Divorce*

Divorce is not an event, but a journey. Remember that no two individuals or families go through this transformation exactly the same way, and that it is rare for anyone to experience just one stage at a time.

1. Before the Breakup
FEELINGS: The loss or absence of love, yet continued attachment. Denial, tension, ambivalence, and self-doubt. Depression, anger, fear, dread, guilt, self-blame, blaming. Desperation and hope.

ACTIONS: Endless arguments. Putting things off, distancing, fighting and making up, soul-searching, keeping secrets, complaining, acting-out, provocation, outbursts, threats, lack of energy, physical symptoms, an often unconscious or unspoken game of "hot potato" concerning who will take the ultimate step.

RECOMMENDATIONS: Face up to what is going on, communicate your feelings and needs. If possible, make a mutual commitment to reaching a decision together. Get couple counseling. Although it may be very painful, keep your spouse informed about what you are doing and going through—*secrets and surprises can be extremely destructive.*

2. Separating
FEELINGS: Relief, euphoria, confusion, panic, acute anxiety, "overwhelmed." Betrayal, despair, anger, bitterness, resentment, shock, denial, numbness. Identity confusion.

---

*Constance Ahrons and Roy H. Rodgers (*Divorced Families: A Multidisciplinary View*), Isolina Ricci (*Mom's House, Dad's House*), and Robert S. Weiss (*Marital Separation*) all clarified my understanding of the divorce transition.

ACTIONS: Physical separation; arguments; scrambling to establish temporary home; money problems; multiple, rapid changes; telling/not telling others; dealing with the reactions of others; attempts (often through extreme acting-out) to re-establish the old relationship.

RECOMMENDATIONS: Give your spouse and children ample warning and explanation. Separate from your spouse, but stay close to your children. Take one step at a time. Reach out to realistic, supportive family and friends. Get supportive counseling. Get legal advice. Avoid impulse actions and reactions. Prioritize, deal with the basics first. If you are the initiator, help your spouse to understand, to catch up to you, perhaps through couple counseling.

3. Crazy Time

FEELINGS: Intense feelings of hope and despair, euphoria and sadness, relief and bitterness, mourning, sadness, self-blame, blaming, anger, hatred, neediness, tenderness. Feeling threatened, "stressed out," out-of-control.

ACTIONS: Intrusive memories, reconciling and breaking up again, loss of energy or too much energy, compulsive activities, sleeplessness, loss of appetite or overeating, new involvements, angry exchanges, arguments, threats, fights, loss of control, impulsive or manipulative moves, relationships, or outbursts, illness, in some cases "negative reconstruction of spousal identity," violence, child stealing, abuse.

RECOMMENDATIONS: Be careful! Don't make major decisions needlessly or impulsively. Talk openly and a lot with reliable friends and advisors. Set up a program to take care of yourself physically and emotionally. Make sure that your children's needs are being met. Go slowly with new relationships, geographical moves, etc. Get individual counseling. Get a good, family-oriented attorney. Give yourself, your children, and your ex a lot of leeway—none of you is acting anywhere near your best. Work to establish clear boundaries between yourself and your ex-spouse.

4. A New Beginning

FEELINGS: Realistic hopes and fears, increasing self-esteem, increasing perspective on your old relationship, increasing comfort with your new life and your new identity, episodic sadness, reminiscence, longing, anger, etc.

ACTIONS: Negative intimacy evolves into neutrality, friendship, or a businesslike relationship. You can now see both good and bad aspects of the old relationship, see responsibility and blame on both sides. You may be experimenting with new involvements; forming a new, individual identity; developing your own style in terms of parenting, work, or school; new friendships, new relationships. You may be increasingly able to negotiate with your ex-spouse, solve problems in a businesslike way.

RECOMMENDATIONS: Be open to new ideas and experiences. Work to build a businesslike relationship with your ex-spouse. Clarify those areas of your life that are separate and those, involving the children, that continue to be shared. Make a real home for yourself and the children. Make plans, take steps to get on with your life. Mediation and negotiation may be of help in finalizing the financial, legal, and parenting aspects of your divorce. Be willing to experiment with parenting plans, other aspects of your life.

5. A New Identity

FEELINGS: Renewed security, sense of well-being, self-esteem, optimism, enjoyment, and love.

ACTIONS: Problem solving via businesslike relationship with ex-spouse, investment of energies in new lifestyle, building new relationship, stable parenting arrangements, having fun again.

RECOMMENDATIONS: Solve problems, move ahead, give of yourself, work to maintain a businesslike relationship with ex-spouse despite changes (e.g., moving, remarriage), relax, enjoy.

Suggested Readings

Books about Divorce

AHRONS, CONSTANCE R., and ROY H. RODGERS.
Divorced Families: A Multidisciplinary Developmental View. New York: Norton, 1987.

Presents research and theory about families going through the separation-divorce-remarriage transition. Develops the concept of the binuclear family, and explores the differences between parents who make this transition cooperatively or with ongoing conflict.

GARDNER, R. A.
Child Custody Litigation: A Guide for Parents and Mental Health Professionals. Cresskill, NJ: Creative Therapeutics, 1986.

Substantiates the author's strong warning against the effect of litigation and litigious lawyers on custody cases. Labels and describes the "parental alienation syndrome." Advocates a focus on which parent most thoroughly met the child's early developmental needs.

————. *The Parents' Book about Divorce.* New York: Bantam, 1979.

Practical advice covering many important issues.

GOLDSTEIN, S., and A. J. SOLNIT.
Divorce and Your Child: Practical Suggestions for Parents. New Haven: Yale University Press, 1984.

Sensible, although somewhat dry and simplified overview of the divorce-custody process.

KRANTZLER, MEL.
Creative Divorce. New York: New American Library, 1974.
Presents divorce as an opportunity for personal growth, describes stages of divorce, and offers many useful ideas for divorcing men and women.

LUEPNITZ, D. A.
Child Custody: A Study of Families After Divorce. Lexington, MA: D. C. Heath, 1982.
A thorough and useful report of a study comparing maternal, paternal, and joint custody families.

MCGUIRE, PAULA.
Putting It Together: Teenagers Talk about Family Breakups. New York: Delacorte, 1987.
Interviews with teenagers mixed with comments by professionals give this book a nitty-gritty, honest quality.

MEYERS, SUSAN, and JOAN LAKIN.
Who Will Take the Children: A New Custody Option for Divorcing Mothers and Fathers. New York: Bobbs-Merrill, 1983.
The authors deal honestly with the issues faced by noncustodial mothers. Should be read by women and men who must make a custody decision.

STEARNS, ANN KAISER.
Living through Personal Crisis. New York: Ballantine, 1984.
Not specifically about the divorce crisis, but a very well-written and insightful book.

TRAFFORD, ABIGAIL.
Crazy Time: Surviving Divorce. New York: Bantam Books, 1984.
A gutsy, nitty-gritty, first-person view of divorce and how to get through it intact.

WALKER, GLYNNIS.
Solomon's Children: Exploding the Myths of Divorce. New
York: Arbor House, 1986.
Based on questionnaires answered by over three hundred
and fifty children of divorce, this book is full of firsthand
information. It conveys the resilience of people dealing with
divorce, and states a strong case for full involvement by both
parents.

WALLERSTEIN, J. A., and J. B. KELLY.
*Surviving the Break-up: How Children and Parents Cope
with Divorce.* New York: Basic Books, 1980.
A must for anyone who wants to look more deeply into the
effects of divorce. An excellently written, factual, and
insightful report on a clinically oriented long-term study of
divorcing families.

WEITZMAN, L. J.
*The Divorce Revolution: The Unexpected Social and
Economic Consequences for Women and Children in America.*
New York: The Free Press, 1985.
Weighty, but excellent research-based book detailing the
financial and social inequities that have followed from the
current application of no-fault divorce legislation.

Books about Shared Parenting
GALPER, M. A.
*Joint Custody and Co-Parenting: Sharing Your Child
Equally.* Philadelphia: Running Press, 1980.
Pages of interviews with parents who have worked out their
custody problems on their own make this book very real. An
excellent sourcebook for parents.

MORGENBESSER, M., and N. NEHLS.
Joint Custody. Chicago: Nelson-Hall, 1981.
A short how-to book, written in nontechnical language.
Includes extensive references, some historical background,

guidelines, and approaches to special problems and issues. Has some revealing interviews with parents and children.

Ricci, I.
Mom's House, Dad's House: Making Shared Custody Work. New York: Macmillan, 1980.
Excellent workbook on why and how to make joint custody work. An accessible and useful book for parents, to whom it consistently gives constructive guidance and practical help.

Ware, Ciji.
Sharing Parenthood after Divorce: An Enlightened Custody Guide for Mothers, Fathers and Children. New York: Bantam Books, 1984.
A thorough and useful guide for parents. Has many practical checklists, forms, and other resources.

Wooley, Persia.
The Custody Handbook. New York: Summit Books, 1979.
Surveys many different kinds of child custody arrangements, focusing on shared responsibility for the children.

Yours, Mine, and Ours

Berman, Claire.
Making It as a Stepparent: New Roles/New Rules. New York: Doubleday, 1980.
Easy reading, down-to-earth, and very practical.

Ephron, Delia.
Funny Sauce: Us, the Ex, the Ex's New Mate, the New Mate's Ex, and the Kids. New York: Viking, 1986.
This witty and insightful book conveys a lot of personal experience in a delightful way.

Paris, Erna.
Stepfamilies: Making Them Work. New York: Avon, 1984.
Provides basic information and many practical suggestions for parents in blended families. Presented in a lively, readable, and refreshing style.

VISHER, EMILY, and JOHN VISHER.
Stepfamilies: Myths and Realities. New York: Lyle Stuart,
1980.
Presents a realistic view of extended and blended families,
with some useful ideas on how to make them work better.

About Negotiation and Mediation
BIENENFELD, FLORENCE.
*Child Custody Mediation: Techniques for Counselors,
Attorneys and Parents.* Palo Alto, CA: Science and Behavior
Books, 1983.
Straightforward manual on mediation by an experienced
conciliation court counselor.

BLADES, JOAN.
Family Mediation: Cooperative Divorce Settlement.
Englewood Cliffs, NJ: Prentice-Hall, 1985.
Excellent, up-to-date book for professionals and parents
interested in divorce mediation. Includes useful transcripts,
forms, and sample agreements.

COHEN, HERB.
You Can Negotiate Anything. New York: Bantam, 1982.
This breezy best-seller can help anyone to become a more
confident and competent negotiator.

FISHER, ROGER, and WILLIAM URY.
Getting to Yes: Negotiating Agreement without Giving In.
New York: Penguin Books, 1981.
A brief, but powerful guide to principled negotiation.

IRVING, HOWARD H.
Divorce Mediation: The Rational Alternative. Toronto:
Personal Library Publishers, 1980.
Written for laypeople and professionals, this book presents
a constructive approach to mediation.

JANDT, FRED E., and PAUL GILLETTE.
Win-win Negotiating: Turning Conflict into Agreement. New York: Wiley, 1985.
An excellent and practical workbook for developing your negotiating and mediating skills.

Legal Matters

CLAIR, BERNARD, and ANTHONY DIANIELI.
The Ex-Factor: The Complete Do-It-Yourself Post-Divorce Handbook. New York: Warner Books, 1987.
Contains useful legal information about enforcement and modification of support, visitation, and custody issues.

FRIEDMAN, JAMES T.
The Divorce Handbook: Your Basic Guide to Divorce. New York: Random House, 1982.
Full of checklists, guides, and worksheets, this book provides clear answers to many of the questions a parent might have about the legalities of divorce.

GERHARD, F. J., JR.
The Illinois Do-It-Yourself Divorce Kit. Chicago: Contemporary Books, 1984.
Clarifies Illinois divorce law and procedures for parents.

GIBONEY, DANIEL W.
So You Want a Divorce: How to Do It Yourself in the State of Washington. D. Giboney: 1984.
Presents Washington divorce law and procedures for parents.

GRUMET, ROBERT.
How to Do Your Own Divorce in Nevada. Las Vegas: Utopia Press, 1983.
Summarizes Nevada divorce law and procedures for parents.

MALOY, RICHARD H.
Your Questions Answered about Florida Divorce Law. Miami: Windward Publications, 1984.

_____. *Your Continuing Obligations after Divorce.* Miami: Windward Publications, 1978.
These books clarify Florida divorce law for parents.

MARAN, MICHAEL.
The Michigan Divorce Book: A Guide to Doing an Uncontested Divorce without an Attorney (with Minor Children). East Lansing, MI: Grand River Press, 1986.
Describes Michigan divorce law and procedures for parents.

MATTHEWS, JOSEPH L., MARY WILLIS, and WARREN SIEGEL.
How to Modify and Collect Child Support in California. Berkeley, CA: Nolo Press, 1987.
Gives a very clear picture of the legal steps for changing support after a divorce is finalized.

McCONAUGHEY, DAN E.
Georgia Handbook on Divorce, Alimony and Child Custody: Revised Layman's Edition. Norcross, GA: Harrison Co., 1981.
Clarifies Georgia divorce and child custody law for parents.

SHERMAN, CHARLES E.
How to Do Your Own Divorce (current California edition). Berkeley, CA: Nolo Press.
These books make the law and legal procedures as clear as they can be for divorcing parents.

SHERMAN, CHARLES E., and JIM SIMONS.
How to Do Your Own Divorce in Texas. Berkeley, CA: Nolo Press, 1983.
Summarizes Texas divorce law and procedures for parents.

WHEELER, MICHAEL.
Divided Children: A Legal Guide for Divorcing Parents. New York: W.W. Norton, 1980.
A clear and thoughtful exploration of the legalities of custody, written for parents.

Books for Children

Bienenfeld, Florence.

My Mom and Dad are Getting a Divorce. St. Paul: EMC, 1980. Available by mail from EMC Corp., 180 E. 60th St., St. Paul, MN 55101.

This illustrated book brings out key issues and helps children ages three through eight deal with the emotional impact of divorce.

Blume, Judy.

It's Not the End of the World. New York: Dell, 1986.

Sensitive, insightful, and honest. For older children and early teenagers.

Brown, Laurene Krasny, and Marc Tolon Brown.

Dinosaurs Divorce: A Guide for Changing Families. New York: Atlantic Monthly, 1986.

The dinosaur illustrations and a great sense of humor work wonders to cushion the hurt of an insightful look at divorce for children four through eight or older.

Cleary, Beverly.

Dear Mr. Henshaw. New York: Dell, 1984.

For eight- to twelve-year-olds. A boy's letters to a favorite author reveal his problems with his parents' divorce.

Danziger, Paula.

The Divorce Express. New York: Dell, 1986.

For children twelve and older. A girl resents her parents' divorce, but tries to find a new place for herself in their new lives.

Dragonwater, Crescent.

Always, Always. New York: Macmillan, 1984.

For children five through nine. A little girl discovers that her parents' divorce does not diminish their love for her.

Gardner, Richard A.

The Boys and Girls Book about Divorce. New York: Bantam Books, 1971.

This book for children eight and older helps them cope
with many issues, including anger at their divorcing parents.

GROLLMAN, EARL A.
Talking about Divorce and Separation. Boston: Beacon
Press, 1975.
A good book with illustrations for children and well-
organized guidelines for parents.

HELMERING, DORIS.
I Have Two Families. New York: Abingdon, 1981.
For children four through nine. A girl describes her feelings
about her parents' divorce and her two homes.

KREMENTZ, JILL.
How It Feels When Parents Divorce. New York: Knopf,
1984
Children seven through sixteen share their feelings about
divorce.

LESHAN, EDA.
*What's Going to Happen to Me? When Parents Separate or
Divorce.* New York: Aladdin Books, 1986.
Highly recommended book for children ten and older.

MAGID, KEN, and WALT SCHREIBMAN.
Divorce Is . . .: A Kids' Coloring Book. Gretna, LA:
Pelican Publishing Company, 1980.
Helps younger children deal with twenty-five divorce-
related problems through entertaining cartoons of problems
and their solutions.

MOORE, EMILY.
Something to Count On. New York: Dutton, 1980.
For older children and teenagers. A ten-year-old girl's
behavior at school worsens because of family problems, but
she is helped by an understanding teacher.

RICHARDS, ARLENE, AND IRENE WILLIS.
*How to Get It Together When Your Parents Are Coming
Apart.* New York: David McKay, 1976.

This book can be useful for teenagers dealing with their parents' divorce. It encourages them to voice their preferences concerning which parent they want to live with.

Thomas, Marlo.
Free to Be . . . a Family. New York: Bantam, 1987.
Just as *Free to Be . . . You and Me* challenged racial and sexist stereotypes, this book and album by Marlo Thomas and Friends tells children, "Whatever your family is is a family."

Voight, Cynthia.
A Solitary Blue. New York: Macmillan, 1983.
For children twelve and older. A boy's mother returns after years of separation, creating a rift between him and his father that takes love and honesty to heal.

Books about Children
Briggs, Dorothy C.
Your Child's Self-Esteem. New York: Dolphin Books, 1975.
Although not about children of divorce specifically, this book is basic reading for divorced parents. It gives very detailed information about child development and behavior.

List, Julie.
The Day the Loving Stopped. New York: Fawcett, 1981.
An insightful and moving account of the potential effects of divorce on children.

Teyber, Edward.
Helping Your Children with Divorce: A Compassionate Guide for Parents. New York: Pocket Books, 1985.
Gives practical advice not only concerning children's fears, fantasies, and conflicts, but also concerning parental cooperation and parenting skills.

Men and Fathering
Dodson, Fitzhugh.
How to Father. New York: New American Library, 1974.
A classic full of insights and advice about every aspect of being a father.

GATLEY, RICHARD H.
Single Father's Handbook. New York: Anchor Books, 1979.
A very helpful book about being a good father and a cooperative coparent after divorce.

GREIF, GEOFFREY L.
Single Fathers. Lexington, MA: D. C. Heath, 1985.
Although written primarily for professionals working with single fathers, this book is full of useful information and insights into single fatherhood.

ROMAN, M., and W. HADDAD.
The Disposable Parent: The Case for Joint Custody. New York: Holt, Rinehart & Winston, 1978.
A source book on the father's role and importance in children's lives after divorce. Combines a study of custodial and visiting fathers with advocacy of shared custody.

ROSENTHAL, KRISTINE M., and HARRY F. KESHET.
Fathers without Partners: A Study of Fathers and the Family after Marital Separation. Totowa, NJ: Rowman & Allanheld, 1981.
Solid background material, a careful study of 129 custodial fathers, with many practical recommendations.

SPIEGEL, LAWRENCE D.
A Question of Innocence: A True Story of False Accusation. Parsippany, NJ: Unicorn Publishing House, 1986.
A gripping personal account of a father's defense against false charges of abusing his daughter. Concludes with practical suggestions and advice.

Women and Mothering
The Custody Handbook: A Woman's Guide to Child Custody Disputes. Available from the Women's Legal Defense Fund, 2000 P Street, N.W., Suite 400, Washington, DC 20036.

Gillis, Phyllis L.
Days Like This: A Tale of Divorce. New York: McGraw, 1986.

An intense personal account of a woman who came to see divorce as essentially a business transaction in which the woman often loses. Frank, with much sound advice.

Hootman, Marcia, and Patt Perkins.
How to Forgive Your Ex-Husband (and Get on with Your Life). New York: Warner Books, 1985.

Has many good ideas for working through negative emotional attachments.

Hope, Karol, and Nancy Young (eds.).
MOMMA: The Sourcebook for Single Mothers. New York: New American Library, 1976.

Full of factual material and personal accounts of single mothers (and fathers).

Rutter, Michael.
The Qualities of Mothering: Maternal Deprivation Reassessed. New York: Jason Aronson, 1974.

A serious assessment of the mother-child bonding process and its importance throughout life.

Women in Transition: A Feminist Handbook on Separation and Divorce. New York: Scribner's, 1975.

Practical and with many resource listings and addresses. It discusses emotional support, children, legal issues, and economics.

Index

249

About the Author

Robert E. Adler, Ph.D., is a clinical psychologist with fifteen years of experience in family counseling. He currently practices in Santa Rosa, California, where the majority of his work is with divorced and divorcing families. He presents frequent workshops for parents, attorneys, and mental health professionals, and has found in his workshops that parents and professionals react favorably to the ideas embodied in *Sharing the Children*.

ABOUT THE MAKING OF THIS BOOK

The text of *Sharing the Children*
was set in Times Roman by
Pagesetters, Inc., of Brattleboro,
Vermont. The book was printed and
bound by the Maple-Vail Book
Manufacturing Group of
Binghamton, New York. The
typography and binding were
designed by Tom Suzuki of Falls
Church, Virginia.

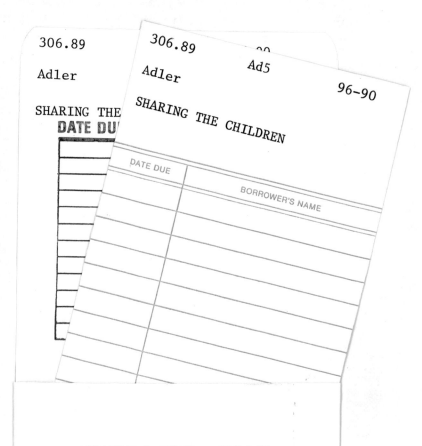

306.89

Adler

SHARING THE
DATE DUE

306.89   Ad5

Adler   96-90

SHARING THE CHILDREN

DATE DUE   BORROWER'S NAME